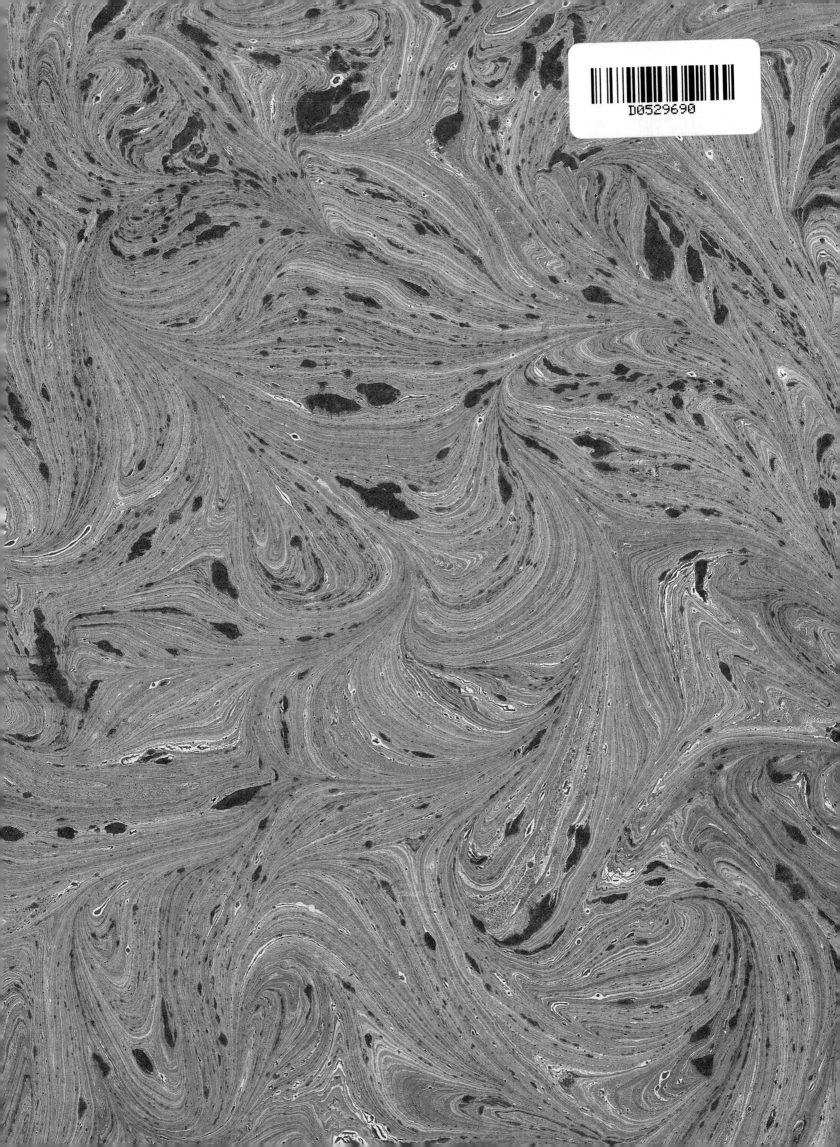

Holiday Homes

Holiday Homes

Compiled by Nancy J. Fitzpatrick   Written by Vicki L. Ingham

Oxmoor House

Southern Living® HOLIDAY HOMES
from the *At Home with Southern Living* series

©1991 by Oxmoor House, Inc.
Book Division of Southern Progress Corporation
P.O. Box 2463, Birmingham, Alabama 35201

Library of Congress Number: 91-062C23
ISBN: 0-8487-0746-X
Manufactured in the United States of America

SECOND EDITION

Executive Editor: Nancy J. Fitzpatrick
Director of Manufacturing: Jerry R. Higdon
Production Manager: Rick Litton
Art Director: Bob Nance
Copy Chief: Mary Jean Haddin

Editor: Vicki L. Ingham
Senior Designer: Cynthia Rose Cooper
Contributing Editors: Kathleen English, Margaret
Allen Northen; Carole Engle, Homes Editor, and
Linda Hallam, Building Editor, *Southern Living*
magazine
Assistant Editor: Heidi Tyline King
Editorial Assistant: Shannon Sexton
Production: Theresa L. Beste, Pam Beasley Bullock

*Special thanks to Charles Maloy Love for his assistance with
"Portfolio of Techniques."
Marbleized paper by Julie Wilson.*

Contents

Introduction

AN ENGLISHMAN WHO HAD SPENT CHRISTMAS IN Virginia wrote in a 1746 issue of *London Magazine* that "All over the Colony, an universal Hospitality reigns; full Tables and open Doors, the kind Salute, the generous Detention, speak somewhat like the old Roast-beef Ages of our Fore-fathers. . . . Strangers are fought after with Greediness, as they pass the Country, to be invited."

Hospitality is still a Southern specialty, one that is practiced with particular exuberance at Christmas. A table full of good food continues to be the centerpiece of festivities, but now the open door is framed with greenery and the hall inside is decorated with arrangements of fruits, nuts, ribbons, and flowers. Decorations have become an eloquent way of welcoming the season, setting the stage for celebration.

That kind of stage set—the focus of this book— is a fairly recent innovation, but the conviviality it expresses is a long-standing Southern tradition. Massachusetts, settled by Puritans, banned all festivity at Christmas, regarding it as a dangerous survival of pagan customs. But in Maryland, where there were large numbers of Roman Catholics, and Virginia, with a fair number of Episcopalians, Christmas was observed with enthusiasm. By 1709, the celebrations started on December 15 and continued until January 6, with Christmas observed on January 5. (The date was changed in 1750.)

William Byrd II of Westover, in Virginia, recorded in his diary that Christmas Day began with a breakfast of broiled turkey, followed by attendance at church and an evening of merrymaking. This could involve billiards, wine drinking, card playing, ice skating, and feasting. In some Southern states, including Alabama, Maryland, Kentucky, and West Virginia, the day was observed with firecrackers, shooting of guns, fox hunts, and day-long visits to neighbors and friends for eggnog, a huge meal, and dancing.

Exchanging gifts was not an important part of colonial Christmases, but churches were decorated with greenery. According to one newspaper description written in 1712, "the pews look like so many arbours. . . . The pulpit itself has such clusters of ivy, holly and rosemary about it that a light fellow in our pew took occasion to say that the congregation heard the 'Word out of the bush, like Moses.' " Documentary evidence suggests that homes were also decorated with boughs of evergreens. Fruits, candies, and an array of special dishes were decorative, too, at least until they were eaten.

According to Harnett Kane, author of *The Southern Christmas Book*, the Christmas tree entered Southern tradition via Williamsburg. A young German named Charles Frederic Ernest Minnegerode came to Virginia to teach Greek and Latin at William and Mary College. He became good friends with the family of a fellow professor, Judge Nathaniel Tucker, and in 1842 introduced to them the custom of bringing a fir tree indoors and decorating it with candles, popcorn strings, and paper ornaments. German immigrants had brought the custom to the Northeast even earlier and took it with them as they moved west—by 1862, Christmas

trees were found even in San Francisco. According to German practice, the trees were small and stood on tabletops; but after 1860, floor-to-ceiling trees, a uniquely American innovation, began gaining favor.

Trees, gift-giving, caroling, and Christmas cards all became part of Christmas celebrations in the Victorian era. The Victorians also invented notions about Christmas that still prevail today. Washington Irving and Charles Dickens conjured in their novels images of Christmases past that were pure fiction; but these images took hold of the Victorian imagination and became firmly rooted in the middle class mind as the picture of what Christmas once was and was meant to be: a celebration of human sympathy, childhood innocence, family ties and warm feelings, blazing fires in great halls, lots of family, cousins, friends, plenty of food and drink for all. It was the epitome of the Victorian celebration of home and family, balanced by philanthropy and attention to the poor.

These ideas about what Christmas should be continue to find expression in the way we celebrate. What are the succession of open houses and parties we plan but a way to enjoy the gifts of friendship? The piles of presents that accumulate in the spare bedroom affirm the ties of kith and kin. And the decorations that transform the house inside and out bring on a mood of festivity.

It's the decorations that are the subject of this book. Carols and Christmas music may trigger feelings of anticipation and excitement, and the aromas of cakes and cookies baking may stir up childhood memories of only-at-Christmas treats. But it's the wreath on the door, the Nativity on the mantel, the ornament-laden tree in the family room that emphatically declare Christmas is here.

As tradition-rich as the season is, it also spurs creative people to look for new ways to dress the house in what amounts to party clothes. Creativity is

like a chain reaction—one clever idea sparks another. When you see a garland of lemons at a house museum in Maryland, a mantel decorated with curling ribbon and grapevine in a Houston residence, or a kissing ball made of boxwood and cranberries in Williamsburg, you come away with ideas for imbuing your own home with a festive atmosphere. "Holiday Heritage" presents a selection of Southern houses noteworthy for their historic or architectural interest and decorated for the season. "Home for the Holidays" takes you into private residences around the region. "Festive Focus" looks closely at the areas of the house that are most likely to be decorated

or where decorations will have the most impact: the front door, the entrance hall and stairs, the dining room, mantels, and of course, the tree. In addition to explanations of how these decorations were assembled, there are step-by-step illustrations of basic methods for making garlands, wreaths, and badges in the final chapter, "Portfolio of Techniques."

The styles and approaches to decorating presented in *Holiday Homes* range from brilliantly unconventional to richly traditional, and arrangements reflect the talents of both professional designers and gifted amateurs. Throughout, the Southern spirit of high celebration reigns.

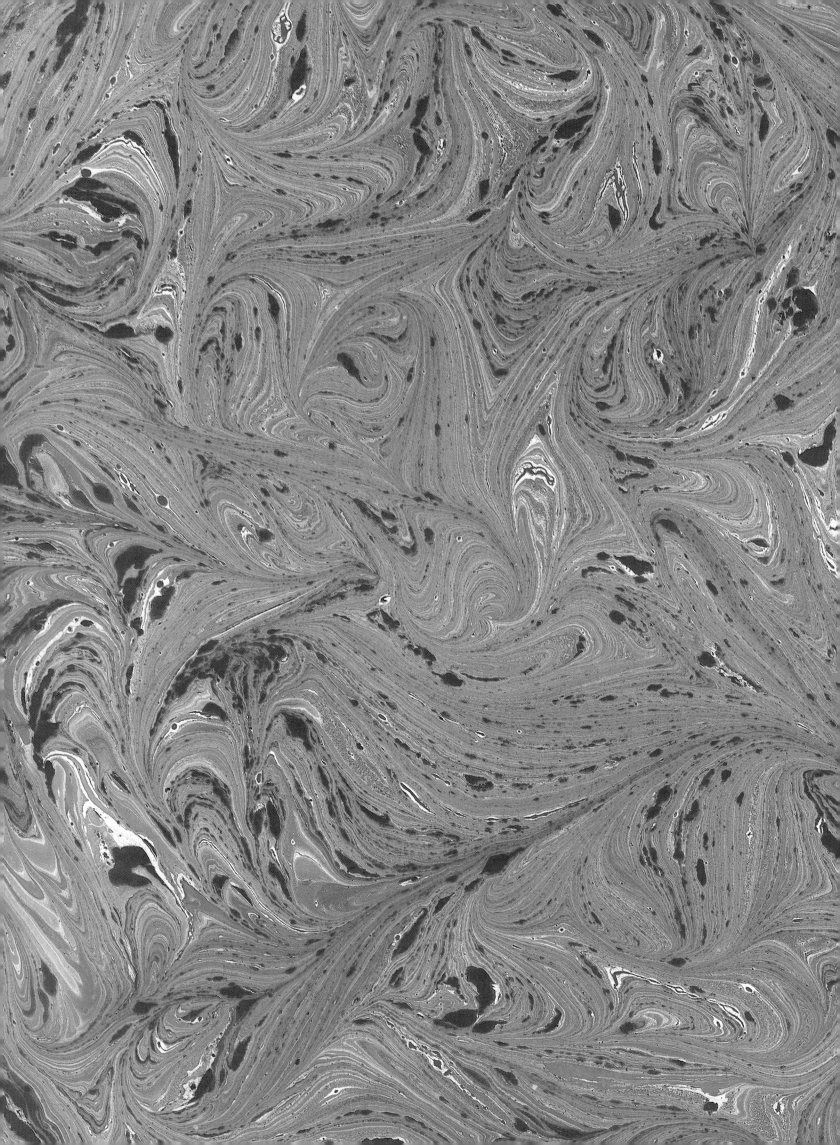

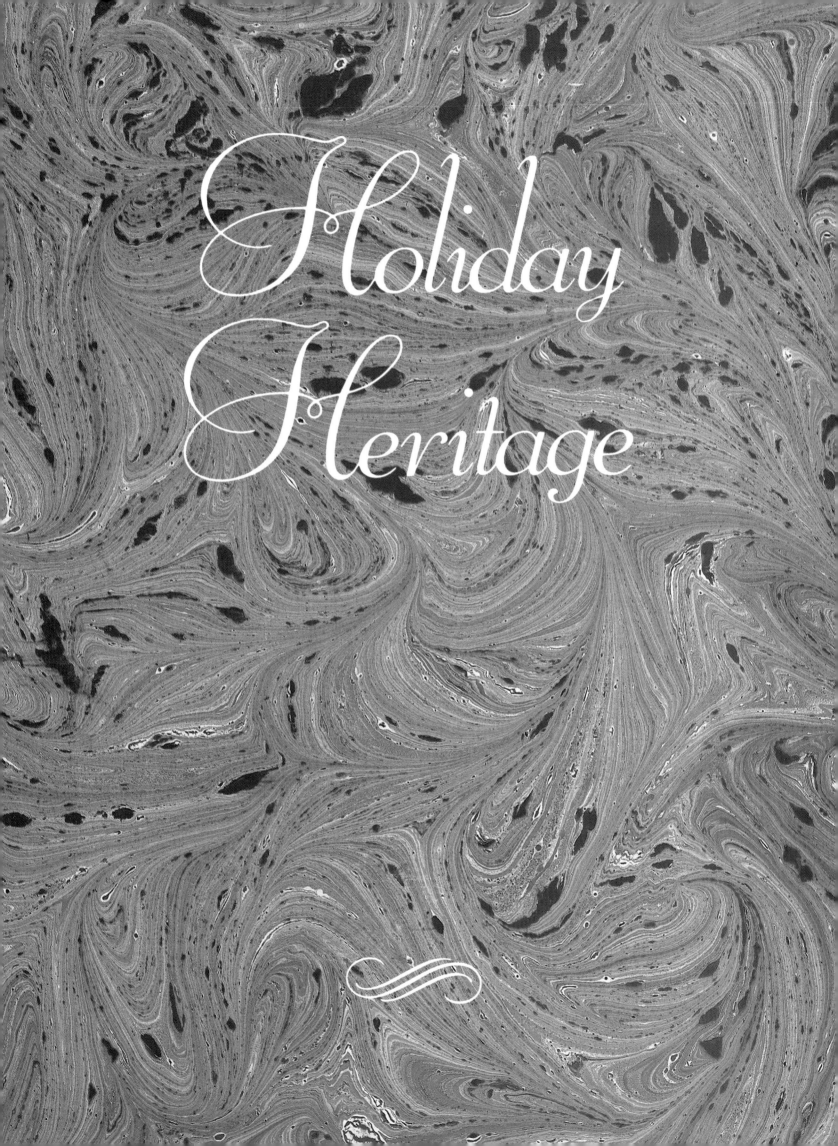

Holiday Heritage

William Paca House

WILLIAM PACA "WAS A HANDSOME MAN, MORE THAN six feet high, of portly appearance," wrote artist Charles Willson Peale, who had ample opportunity to study his subject while working on a portrait of Paca. "Being well educated and accustomed to the best company, he was graceful in his movements and complacent to everyone; in short his manners were of the first polish." There was more to Paca than good looks and good manners, however. A member of Maryland's wealthy, educated elite, he participated in the Continental Congress, signed the Declaration of Independence, served as governor of Maryland, and was both a state and a federal judge.

In choosing a life of public service, Paca followed the example of his father, an affluent planter who held a variety of elected and appointed offices in Baltimore County. Because his elder brother would inherit the family land, Paca was sent to school in Philadelphia to prepare for a profession. During his second year at the College of Philadelphia, he probably read Isaac Ware's translation of Andrea Palladio's *Four Books of Architecture* (it was part of the students' suggested extra reading). Gentlemen were expected to be well versed on architecture, and the house that Paca would begin building in Annapolis in 1763 would show the influence of his reading.

In 1760, Paca went to London to study law at the Inns of Court. There was tremendous status attached to attending what was then "the most important legal center in the English-speaking world," and few colonial lawyers enjoyed the privilege.

When he returned to Annapolis, he met Ann Mary Chew, who was six years older than he and sought after by all of the eligible bachelors. She could choose whom she pleased: her family was rich and her social connections were impeccable, with relationships by blood or marriage to nearly every important family in Maryland. She chose William, and it was with her money that the couple bought two lots on Prince George Street four days after their wedding. The two-story brick town house that they built was a model of Georgian

Exemplifying the middle- to late-Georgian style, the Paca House has flat arches over the windows and a flat, plain facade.

simplicity, harmony, and symmetry.

The Pacas moved into the house in 1765, and over the next nine years they entertained often and well. Although Christmas did not have the sentimental significance that it would acquire in the next century, it was observed in Annapolis with church-going and feasting. The harbor was one of the busiest on the east coast, and markets offered imported fruits such as lemons, oranges, pineapples, pomegranates, and mangoes, as well as English cheeses, tea, and coffee. Holiday menus in Annapolis homes would surpass the already-generous table laid for guests on other occasions and might include roast

Boxwood roping and lemons swag the staircase in the entry. The lemons are strung on fishing line, using a large darning needle, and the line is knotted between each lemon. The arrangement on the table repeats the yellow and green theme, with boxwood, leucothoe, variegated English holly, eucalyptus, dried yarrow, and fresh lemons. The portrait at the head of the stairs is of Henrietta Maria, wife of Charles I of England, for whom the state is named.

duck, meat pie, chilled oysters, decorative cakes, dried fruit, cranberry sauce, Madeira and burgundy jellies, and pumpkin pudding.

A heavily laden table was the focus of Yuletide entertaining, but Mary Paca may have added to the festive atmosphere by decorating the house with greenery. Her husband developed a magnificent garden that stretched from the back of the house to the Severn River, and it offered boxwood and holly as well as other evergreens. Citrus would have served as both decoration and dessert, as would the grapes, apples, and pears grown on the plantation in the country and stored in barrels of sawdust for winter use.

Mary Paca died on January 15, 1774, leaving William with three children. After her death, Paca spent little time in the Annapolis town house and finally sold it in 1780. Today, it is maintained by Historic Annapolis Foundation and is one of the city's finest historic house museums. At Christmas, volunteers prepare festive foods, using pre-Revolutionary War recipes. Docents and members of the William Paca Garden Guild decorate the house to reflect the

The trimwork in the parlor is the most elaborate in the house, done ten years after the structure was completed in 1765. The bright blue wall color is authentic, verified by chemical analysis of paint samples. The mantel decoration is based on a design published in the eighteenth century by architect Batty Langley. The acorns have been varnished, pierced, and wired into clusters and then secured to a rope of evergreens.

way the people of Annapolis celebrated the season in the late 1780s. The decorations are authentic in that only those plant materials are used that are known to have been available at the time: English and American holly and boxwood, English and Irish yew, English ivy, leucothoe, pine, magnolia, bayberry, and cranberries could all be found in Anne Arundel County, and the fruits and nuts would have been available in the city.

The William Paca House is open to the public year round, but the special candlelight tours at Christmas may be the best way to experience the house as William and Mary Paca knew it.

The dining table arrangement is a twentieth-century interpretation of a plateau, a French treatment that was popular in the early 1700s. A hedge of boxwood in blocks of florists' foam outlines the mirror base. Marzipan fruits and fish are then placed on the hedge, and narrow satin ribbons curl loosely from the central candlestick to the greenery.

Hammond-Harwood House

Twin wreaths decorate the front door of the Hammond-Harwood House. Exquisitely carved with roses and classical motifs, the entry has been described as the most beautiful in the country.

THE YEAR 1773 STARTED WELL FOR MATHIAS Hammond. At age twenty-five, he had just been elected to the Maryland Provincial Assembly and looked forward to a promising political career. And he had just hired the best architect in Annapolis to build a splendid in-town home. Over the next three years, Hammond would be frustrated in politics, but his house would prove to be an architectural triumph, one of the most beautiful houses in colonial America.

The architect, William Buckland, arrived in Virginia in 1755 as a carpenter and joiner indentured to George Mason. By 1771, he was accorded the title of architect and oversaw a shop that included a bricklayer, a carpenter, a painter, and a carver. His work for the Carters and the Tayloes of Virginia and for Edward Lloyd of Wye in Maryland may have commended him to Hammond. Lloyd was Hammond's neighbor in Annapolis, owning a three-story house across from the proposed site of Hammond's new home. The Palladian five-part plan that Buckland designed for Hammond proved to be the architect's masterpiece and has been described as "one of the most perfect examples of Georgian architecture in America today."

That Buckland was thoroughly familiar with the latest architectural styles in England can be inferred from his unusually large library of design and pattern books. Significantly, he seems to have used the books as a guide only; his clients might select a decorative treatment for a bull's-eye window from James Gibbs's *Book of Architecture*, but Buckland would modify the design according to his own sense of style. The plan for Hammond's house consisted of a main two-story block connected to flanking wings by enclosed passages. Proportion and symmetry ruled throughout, to the extent that inside, Buckland installed false doors where necessary to balance real ones. In one respect, the architect deviated from the norm for Maryland mansions: the entry, instead of opening into a large reception hall with stair, leads back to the dining room at the end of the hall. The

emphasis on spacious and elegant rooms for entertaining suggests that the young planter looked forward to hosting his share of the balls, parties, and social events that filled the winter season.

Less than eight months after construction had begun in 1774, the architect suddenly died. Although the residence was completed (probably by John Randall, Buckland's junior partner), Hammond abruptly left Annapolis in 1776 and never lived in his new house. After his death in 1786, it was rented to various tenants. Then Judge Jeremiah Townley Chase bought it for his daughter and her children (he apparently distrusted his son-in-law's ability to provide for them). In a nice bit of irony, the Judge's granddaughter Hester Ann Loockerman

Visitors would have been received in the parlor. This room, to the left of the front door, is arranged for tea, an important social ritual in the eighteenth century. Two Maryland-made Sheraton chairs are drawn up to the Philadelphia tea table, which is set with a blue-and-white Chinese export service. The Baltimore breakfront secretary displays more Chinese export porcelain. Burford holly, apples, pinecones, and juniper dress the mantel beneath the portrait of Mrs. Ninian Pinkney, who once lived in the house.

The kitchen occupies one of the wings and is connected to the main house by an enclosed, brick-floored passage. On the chimney breast, apples alternate with vertical bunches of juniper to form the mantel swag. A fresh juniper wreath with apples, magnolia leaves, and cinnamon sticks is typical of the kind of simple decorations devised for the house at Christmas.

married William Harwood, great-grandson of William Buckland, and the house became home to the architect's descendants.

Since 1938, it has been maintained by the Hammond-Harwood House Association as a historic house museum. Furnished to reflect life in Annapolis during the period 1760 to 1800, the rooms contain eighteenth-century American and English furniture, paintings, and decorative arts, including many of the pieces owned by the Harwoods.

Every Christmas, local garden clubs decorate the house using materials appropriate to the 1700s. Little is known about colonial Christmas decorating customs, except that there would have been no trees, ornaments, or religious symbols. Because Maryland generally followed English practice in celebrating the season, it is likely that local greens and fruits would have been used to create a festive atmosphere in the formal rooms of the house. The garden clubs accommodate twentieth-century expectations by decorating the kitchen as well as the parlor and dining room. But, in keeping with the aesthetics of the era, the designs are simple and symmetrical, a restrained enhancement to one of the most beautiful houses in Annapolis.

Mount Clare

CHARLES CARROLL, LATER TO BE KNOWN AS THE Barrister, spent the first thirty-two years of his life becoming extraordinarily well educated. When he was ten years old, his father took him to Portugal for schooling at the English House in West Lisbon. At age sixteen, he was enrolled at Eton in England and later attended Cambridge. In 1746, he returned to his father's Baltimore County, Maryland, farm, but in 1751 he left for England again to study law at the Inns of Court. Shortly after he returned in 1755,

The Louis XV settee and armchairs, Queen Anne tea table, and painted fire screen furnished the parlor when Charles Carroll, Barrister, and his wife, Margaret Tilghman Carroll, lived here. The plaster walls in this and the other main rooms of the house were made to resemble wood paneling, and deep plaster cornices join walls to ceiling. For Christmas, a formal arrangement of greenery decorates the mantel.

his father died, leaving Carroll an enormous fortune based on iron mines, mills, and a plantation that produced food and tobacco for export.

Carroll stepped easily into his father's shoes. In addition to taking over the family businesses, he was also elected to fill his father's seat in the Lower

House of the Assembly. And he became immersed in the construction of Mount Clare, the country house his father had begun.

Built on a rise above the Patapsco River, the Georgian-style mansion stood about a mile from the river landing. Visitors arriving by boat looked up the hillside to terraced gardens crowned by the spreading, symmetrical structure. From the land approach, the facade of the central block was dominated by a portico of Doric columns imported from England, supporting a second-story pavilion with a Palladian window.

Inside, the plaster walls were molded to look like wood paneling. Adamesque fireplace surrounds in the parlor and dining room were embellished with delicate garlands, urns, and bellflowers. These may have been executed by an Irish craftsman,

The table centerpiece evokes the eighteenth century with fruit and nuts that serve as both decoration and dessert. The 1763 English silver epergne stands on red ribbons that form a St. Andrew's cross. Ivy leaves circle the epergne, and bits of holly accent both the food and the ribbon cross. The English mahogany wine cooler and 1815 Baltimore sideboard are both Carroll pieces. The portraits, attributed to John Hesselius, depict Margaret Tilghman Carroll's grandmother, Anne Grundy Lloyd, and Margaret's cousin, Deborah Lloyd Tilghman.

J. Kennedy, who advertised his skill with "fancy plastering" in the local newspaper.

The house was finally completed in 1763, and in the same year, Carroll married. His bride, Margaret Tilghman of Rich Neck Manor on the Eastern Shore, was almost twenty years younger than her husband. She brought to Mount Clare considerable

horticultural expertise. Under her supervision, the gardener tended orange and lemon trees in the greenhouse and raised broccoli and pineapples in the "pinery." She also advised George Washington on the construction and stocking of his new greenhouse at Mount Vernon.

Carroll's business and political activities often took him to Annapolis, where there were three other Charles Carrolls. To avoid confusion, he was called "the Barrister," reflecting his training at the Inns of Court. Apparently, however, he never actually practiced law. Instead, he put his knowledge to work in service of Anne Arundel County as a member of the Provincial Committee of Correspondence and the Council of Safety. He also sat in the Continental Congress, wrote Maryland's Declaration of Independence, and helped draft the state's first constitution. After independence was won, he was elected to Maryland's first Senate, a post he held until he died on March 23, 1783.

Margaret Carroll survived her husband by thirty-four years. Because the Carrolls' children died in infancy, the bulk of the estate passed to two nephews, James and Nicholas Maccubbin, who assumed the Carroll name in accordance with their uncle's will. By the middle of the nineteenth

In the study, a William and Mary walnut armchair is pulled up to an English Georgian desk and bookcase, ca. 1775. The gold-headed walking stick was the Barrister's, engraved with the Carroll crest. On the mantel, a Washington clock, ca. 1805, is one that Lafayette had made in Paris for presentation to his American friends, a circle that included Charles Carroll, Barrister. Beneath the portrait of his great-nephew, James Carroll, Jr., three small bunches of holly, boxwood, juniper, and dusty miller line the mantel. Similar bouquets are fastened to the fender. The fanlight over the door is emphasized with boxwood secured to a plywood frame that duplicates the design of the window.

century, the city of Baltimore had grown up around Mount Clare, and although the Carroll family continued to own the mansion, they no longer lived in it. Over the next fifty years, it was used as a hotel and a beer garden, then subjected to vandalism and neglect. Finally, in 1890 the heirs sold the property to the city.

Since 1917, the mansion has been maintained as a museum house by the National Society of Colonial Dames of America in the State of Maryland. It is the centerpiece of the 110-acre Carroll Park in

A Colonial-style kitchen was created during the 1960 restoration of the interiors. The furniture and tools date to the eighteenth century.

A trapunto and appliqué quilt made before 1830 dresses the mahogany bed, which was made in Annapolis in 1825. Hepplewhite side chairs, ca. 1780-85, are from a set of six belonging to the Carrolls. The Chippendale wing chair was also the Barrister's. Such chairs allowed the sick to sleep in an upright position.

southwest Baltimore. At Christmas, evergreens, berries, and natural materials that Margaret Carroll might have gathered from her garden are brought indoors to dress the rooms for the holidays. The decorations at Mount Clare are carefully designed to complement the interiors and their furnishings. They capture a sense of the eighteenth century and what the Carrolls would have considered fitting.

Manigault House

JOSEPH MANIGAULT BUILT HIS CHARLESTON, SOUTH Carolina, residence just beyond the city limit in the newly laid-out suburb called Wraggborough. Like the crowded core of the old city, Wraggborough was a commercial and residential neighborhood, but it was still undeveloped enough for Joseph to construct a magnificent house on two lots.

Built around 1803, the house was designed by Joseph's brother, Gabriel, a gentleman amateur architect who, like Thomas Jefferson, taught himself architecture through reading and observation. Gabriel Manigault is also credited with designing the South Carolina Society Hall and Charleston's city hall. Although the three-story residence he drew up for his brother is almost severe in its simplicity on the outside, the interiors reflect the lyrically elegant planning and ornamentation made popular by the Scottish architect and interior designer Robert Adam. Oval and rectangular rooms create a graceful floor plan, and delicate neoclassical motifs decorate the architecture.

An arrangement balanced on the wide cornice above the door lifts the eye to the frieze of urns and swags in the dining room. The dining table, chairs, and sideboards are all Charleston made. The Hepplewhite-style sideboard in the corner is earlier and more typical of Charleston; the painted and stenciled example to the right is in the heavier and more ornate Empire style. On the table, a silver centerpiece by Paul Storr, one of England's master silversmiths, holds a tree made of evergreens, cranberry roping, and fruit. The portrait above the mantel of Peter Manigault, father of the house's owner, is a copy, after the mid-eighteenth-century original by London court painter Allan Ramsay. Peter wrote of this painting, "Tis done by one of the best Hands in England and is accounted by all Judges here, not only an Exceedingly good Likeness, but a very good Piece of Painting."

A garland of pine caught up with red velvet bows emphasizes the graceful ascent of the stair at the Manigault House. The piano, by Charles Albrecht of Philadelphia, is one of the earliest made in America. Above it is a seventeenth-century Italian painting, *The Mystical Marriage of St. Catherine*, which belonged to the Manigault family. Flanking the piano are nineteenth-century Baltimore-made chairs with insets bearing classical figures. According to the administrator of the house, it was not unusual for a Charleston family to have as many as ninety chairs in its inventory.

The Manigaults probably would not have had a Christmas tree, because the custom was not well established in America until the 1840s; but the Garden Club of Charleston has included a small one here to showcase ornaments made with the coiled sweet-grass technique of the Gullah "basket sewers." These artisans continue a tradition of Low Country basket making that is nearly three hundred years old, based on skills the slaves brought with them from West Africa.

Joseph Manigault was the fourth generation of a French Huguenot family whose rise to power and wealth was the stuff of American myth. Judith Giton, fleeing religious persecution in France, arrived in Charleston in 1685. There she met and married Pierre Manigault, who ran a distillery and made whiskey barrels. Their son Gabriel became a successful merchant and, like many of Charleston's elite, shared his fortune through philanthropy. His children, in turn, invested in land and rice, thus ensuring a secure place in Charleston's aristocracy for his grandsons, Joseph and Gabriel. Joseph and his seventy-five-year-old grandfather joined the militia to fight the British during the Revolutionary War, and Joseph and his brother participated in the South Carolina convention to ratify the Constitution in

1788. Through marriage, the Manigaults were allied with the city's other powerful families, the Middletons, Draytons, Izards, and Heywards. Joseph married a Middleton, then, after her death, wed Charlotte Drayton. They raised ten children in the house on Meeting Street before Joseph died in 1843. Now, after many owners, the house has been carefully restored by the Charleston Museum.

Every year at Christmas the Garden Club of Charleston decorates the rooms, using native greenery that would have been available to Charlotte Manigault. It is known that the Manigaults sometimes spent the holiday at their plantation instead of in the city; but because there is no direct documentation of how the family celebrated Christmas, the decorations reflect the talents of the Garden Club rather than an interpretation of period style. The arrangements harmonize well with the interiors, which capture an era of timeless design.

A composition of yew, elaeagnus, nandina berries, and dried hydrangea billows over the mantel's edge in the drawing room, where a Charleston-made satinwood and mahogany tea table is set with Worcester cups and saucers. The Regency sofa and chairs were made in England about 1815 for Thomas Pinckney, minister to Great Britain after the Revolution.

Aiken-Rhett House

WILLIAM AIKEN, JR., AND HIS WIFE, HARRIET, KNEW how to give a good party. In 1851, Frederica Bremer, a Swedish traveler, attended "a great entertainment given by the Governor of South Carolina, Mr. Akin [sic], and his lovely wife. There was very beautiful music; and for the rest, conversation in the room, or out under the piazzas, in the shade of the blossoming creepers, the clematis, the caprifolium, and roses, quite romantic in the soft night air. Five hundred persons, it is said, were invited, and the entertainment was one of the most beautiful I have been present at in this country."

At the time of this musical evening, William Aiken, Jr., was at the height of his political career and on his way to becoming one of the wealthiest men in the state. Born in 1806, he was the only son of William Aiken, Sr., who had emigrated from Northern Ireland as a young man. By the 1820s, the senior Aiken had established himself as a leading cotton merchant and a successful businessman in Charleston. As the first president of the South Carolina Canal and Rail Road Company, William Aiken, Sr., had overseen the construction of a railroad linking Charleston to Hamburg, a newly established South Carolina town opposite Augusta, Georgia. He died in 1831, two years before the line was completed. (When the 136-mile-long track was finished, it was the longest in the world at that time.)

After his father's death, William Aiken, Jr., became director of the Charleston and Hamburg Railroad. He also inherited his father's business interests and a large number of rental properties in Charleston, one of which was a house on the corner of Judith and Elizabeth Streets. It had been built in 1817 by John Robinson, a local merchant, and was a Federal-style, three-story double house on a raised basement. Its main entrance and first- and second-story piazzas faced Judith Street.

Aiken and his new bride decided to make this house their residence and began remodeling it in the fashionable Greek Revival style. The entrance was moved to the Elizabeth Street side, and four wide,

The painting over the mantel, *Romeo and Juliet* by Luther Terry, was acquired on the Aikens' trip to Rome in 1858. The harp is a reminder that Harriet Aiken was an accomplished musician. To make sure that her daughter had music lessons after the war, she sold some of her jewelry to buy a piano that still stands in the drawing room (not shown). Three wall-sized mirrors in gilt frames hang on the east and west ends of this room, and French torchères were placed in front of them to double the illumination of candlelight.

The portrait in pastels over the mantel is of A. Burnet Rhett, one of the five children born to Henrietta Aiken and A. B. Rhett. The child's rocking chair dates to about 1840. The rosy blush of dried hydrangea on the mantel complements the portrait, and beautyberry adds a magenta accent to the magnolia and pine in the fireplace below.

triple-sash windows replaced the ten smaller ones that originally opened from the front rooms onto the piazzas. The two front rooms were now separated by sliding doors of solid mahogany, and a new wing was added for the dining room. New moldings of carved acanthus leaves, anthemia, and Greek-key designs surrounded doors and windows, and black Italian marble mantels replaced the original wood ones. With the renovations under way, the Aikens set off for Europe, returning with crystal and bronze chandeliers, paintings, furniture, and accessories for their new home.

Shortly after the remodeling was completed, Aiken entered politics. He was elected to the state House of Representatives in 1838, to the state Senate in 1842, and to the governorship in 1844. In 1851, the year Frederica Bremer attended the entertainment at his house, he went to Washington, D.C., to serve in the U.S. House of Representatives. He evidently enjoyed considerable respect in Congress, because he was nearly elected Speaker of the House in 1856, losing on the 133rd ballot.

In 1857, the Aikens again traveled to Europe and brought back paintings and sculpture. The new acquisitions and a brief economic boom in the U.S. encouraged a new round of remodeling at the Aikens' house. A picture gallery with a skylight was added, gas jets for lighting were installed, and the third floor was extended over the dining room wing.

By the outbreak of the Civil War, Aiken had retired from political life. He opposed nullification and secession but loyally supported the Confederacy. Jefferson Davis was welcomed as a guest in November 1863. The following year, when Federal troops bombarded the city, Aiken lent his house to the Confederate cause; safely beyond the reach of the shelling, it served as military headquarters for General Pierre G.T. Beauregard.

Before the war, Aiken's rice plantation on Jehossee Island had been quite profitable, but he

Victorian chairs from 1860-75 are pulled up to a marble-topped Empire table, ca. 1810, decorated with a wreath of baby's-breath and dried hydrangea.

Gaslight once illuminated the courtyard-entrance stair. The Charleston Garden Club has given the statue a bouquet of nandina berries and branches of Chinese tallow tree and ringed her pedestal with ivy. In the arch, a Steuben glass vase holds garden greenery.

In the dining room, traces of original wallpaper are visible next to the window, and the whale-oil chandelier is one of two that Harriet Aiken purchased in Paris between 1833 and 1836. The dining table, possibly made by Joseph Meeks of New York, is original to the house.

had always been careful to diversify the sources of his income. Besides having investments in banks and railroads, he helped found the Charleston and Philadelphia Steam Packet Company and the West Point Rice Mill Company, and he may have had investments in Europe as well. Unlike many other Southerners, Aiken survived the war with his fortune intact. He spent the last twenty years of his life helping rebuild the city and contributing to civic affairs, serving as Poor Commissioner for Charleston Neck and trustee of the Peabody Educational Foundation, which provided $3.5 million for education in the South.

The Aikens had two children, a son, who died in infancy, and a daughter, Henrietta, named for William's mother. When Aiken died in 1887, he left the house to Harriet and their daughter, who had married A. Burnet Rhett in 1862.

Now administered by the Charleston Museum, the house is open to the public. Unlike many house museums, it is being preserved in its existing state rather than being restored to an earlier period. Most of the rooms were never electrified, and those that were still have very early wiring that is no longer used. Under the peeling and faded wallpaper in the dining room can be seen the blue flock design of an earlier wallpaper.

Aiken was remembered as "modest and dignified, courageous but not aggressive, firm but unassuming, too broadly intellectual to be harsh in condemnation or extravagant in praise." The house that was his home seems to reflect that same character: there are echoes of elegance without flashiness, an understated, comfortable air of respectability that is almost European in feeling. At Christmas, members of the Charleston Garden Club decorate the house with arrangements that emphasize local greenery and berries. These bring a refreshing, lived-in feeling to rooms filled with a tangible sense of the past.

In 1858, the Aikens added a picture gallery to the house. Niches hold three marble statues, including *Venus of the Bath*, in the style of Canova, by an unknown sculptor. It is reflected in the mirror above the Italian marble mantel. A skylight provided natural illumination for the paintings, which hung salon-style from floor to ceiling.

A nineteenth-century Chinese export vase holds an arrangement of pine, papyrus, magnolia, and philodendron, with nandina berries for color. The painting, by an unknown artist, is typical of the kind tourists bought in Italy in the nineteenth century. The table is also nineteenth-century Italian.

Brompton

AT BROMPTON, IN FREDERICKSBURG, VIRGINIA, THE
sense of history is ever-present: the carefully restored
architectural details, the period and reproduction furnishings, and the battle-scarred brick facade all
evoke the heritage of the house. More than a monument to history, however, it is also a home. As the
residence of the president of Mary Washington College, it serves official functions—into the parlors and
hall William Anderson, Jr., and his wife, Jane, welcome new students and their parents, faculty and
staff, and visiting scholars and speakers. At Christmas, they hold an open house for all faculty and staff
and spouses, a group that has grown over the years to
include about five hundred people. Brompton is also
where the Andersons have raised their three children.
For the community, the sight of soccer goals and bi-
cycles on the lawn has been a novel feature of this
young president's tenure.

When the house was included on a Christmas
tour several years ago, florist Jan Williams, who

White poinsettias, traditional greenery, and touches
of gold complement the Mahal rug and antique French
wallpaper panel in the entrance hall. Wide metallic ribbon
tied around a white pillow, like a package, is one of florist
Jan Williams's favorite ways to turn everyday accessories
into holiday accents.

A live tree stands in the stairwell, part of the original house built in the 1700s. The tree's root ball is wrapped with gold lamé and screened by potted poinsettias and branches of magnolia. Tiny pots of live poinsettias are tucked among the branches as living ornaments (they must be removed and watered every few days). The rich red and gold theme continues up the stairs with velvet and lamé bows and ribbons and bunches of red-dyed baby's-breath.

Warm orange tones in the Gari Melchers painting *Young Fishermen* (ca. 1890) suggested the coppery theme for the mantel decoration. Nandina berries, artichokes, pinecones, coiled sticks, and sea grape leaves have been sprayed with copper paint and combined with pine, holly, and deodar cedar. The modest scale of the design avoids overwhelming the architectural detail of the mantel, which was carved by hand in the eighteenth century and is original to the house.

always decorates for the Andersons, decided that instead of "the same staid eighteenth-century look," she would play up the home's elegance with glittery metallics. Ribbon, spray paint, and unusual materials such as artichokes and sea grape leaves give these decorations a contemporary look. But using them with greenery from the landscape makes them harmonize with the traditional setting.

Although Brompton's builder and the exact date of construction are unknown, a simple four-room structure was standing on the property when George Washington surveyed it in 1752 for his brother-in-law, Fielding Lewis. In 1821, John Lawrence Marye bought the house and surrounding acreage, which became known as Marye's Heights. Over the next twenty years, he enlarged the house to its present size.

Magnolia leaves, boxwood, deodar cedar, and burgundy-painted heather spill out of silver-painted papier mâché cornucopias on the dining table. The fruit and greenery inside the horns of plenty are arranged in florists' foam, but the grapes, apples, strawflowers, and silver-painted ivy leaves are simply placed on the table around them. In the center of the table, a bowl full of florists' foam supports an arrangement of fruit and greenery topped by an ornamental pineapple. On the mantel, deodar cedar, silver pinecones, heather, and matching ribbons embellish the collection of Canton china on loan from the Gari Melchers home, Belmont. The painting between the windows is Melchers's *Sun Porch*, a portrait of English writer-critic C. Lewis-Hind in 1921.

When the Civil War broke out, Brompton's site on Marye's Heights made it the natural choice for Confederate defenses. Troops under the command of General Longstreet manned the heights and on December 13, 1862, successfully turned back General Burnside's army in the First Battle of Fredericksburg. The next year, however, the Second Battle of Fredericksburg ended in a Union victory, and the house was left a "bullet-riddled shell." During the Wilderness and Spotsylvania campaigns in 1864, it was converted to a hospital, and hundreds of wounded lay in the shade of the trees on its lawn. Today, damage from the fighting can still be seen on the brick exterior, and the trenches are visible on the grounds.

After the war, the house became a residence again. Sometime during the last quarter of the nineteenth century, the owner changed the portico, replacing the flat roofline with a gabled one. Too steeply pitched to be a correct Greek Revival pediment, it looks more Victorian than classical and may have been an attempt to update the facade.

The state of Virginia purchased Brompton and 174 acres in 1947 and began restoring the house. Internationally known interior decorator Nancy McClelland supervised the restoration and donated the antique French wallpaper in the entry. Prominently displayed throughout the house are paintings by Gari Melchers, an early twentieth-century artist whose home, studio, and collection of paintings also belong to Mary Washington College. Brompton's downstairs rooms are formal, as you would expect in an official residence with a historic pedigree. But the addition of the Andersons' own furnishings and pictures of their children infuse the house with a lively personal touch.

Oakleigh

ON CHRISTMAS DAY, 1885, THE *DAILY REGISTER* OF Mobile noted that "the Mobile Rifle Company, under the command of Captain Price-Williams, made one parade . . . and presented a fine appearance. The company halted in front of the residence of General T.K. Irwin and presented to the company's sponsor, Miss Daisy Irwin, a basket of flowers."

Today volunteers re-enact this scene at the Irwins' home, Oakleigh, as the culmination of the annual Candlelight Christmas festivities. Since 1955, Oakleigh has been maintained by the Historic Mobile Preservation Society as a historic house museum. And since 1970, "Candlelight Christmas at Oakleigh" has presented a re-creation of Victorian Yuletide, complete with costumed guides.

The house is remarkable architecturally for its distinctive combination of the Greek Revival and raised-cottage styles, grafted onto the T-shaped layout and off-center entrance hall popular in Mobile. While

Oakleigh, above, was built between 1833 and 1838 and exemplifies the distinctive interpretation given to Greek Revival architecture in Mobile. An antique wedding gown in the parlor, left, is part of a special exhibit during "Candlelight Christmas at Oakleigh."

this floor plan was not unique to Mobile, it proved particularly well adapted to the hot, sticky climate because it provided most rooms with excellent cross ventilation. One feature is unique to Oakleigh, however: the exterior cantilevered stair that winds from ground level to the gallery of the main floor. It was apparently the inspiration of the original owner, James W. Roper of Charleston.

In 1831 or 1832, he bought thirty-three acres in what were then the outskirts of Mobile. Before he could begin building, his wife died in childbirth, and his infant daughter died six months later. Nevertheless, in 1833 Roper began directing construction of the house he had designed. Using clay dug on the property, slaves made the bricks for the ground floor walls and square columns supporting the gallery above. The upper story is wood. Originally, the central ground-floor room was used to store cured meats and provisions. Behind it, a cross hall formed the T linking the two wings, one containing the warming kitchen and the other the dining room. Upstairs, the entrance hall ran along one side of the house, from the front to the cross hall at the back. Opening off of it across the front of the house were

double parlors with high ceilings, matching fireplaces, and pocket doors that could be drawn to separate the rooms.

In 1838, Roper completed the house and brought his second wife there to share it with him. Unfortunately, he did not have long to enjoy it. Unable to repay the $20,000 he had borrowed against Oakleigh and nine acres of land, he lost the house to the Bank of the United States in 1840. The bank held the property for twelve years before selling it to Alfred F. Irwin in 1852 for the paltry sum of $4,525. (Irwin and his family may have been renting the house for some time before buying it.)

Irwin's wife, Margaret, who was descended from Irish nobility and was a British citizen, proudly displayed a British flag from Oakleigh's front gallery. When Federal troops arrived in Mobile and began to commandeer private homes for the use of their officers, they decided to avoid offending a subject of the Crown and left the Irwins and their home alone. The Irwins' sympathies were solidly Confederate, of course. Their sons, Thomas Kilshaw and Lee Fearn, both fought in the battle of Atlanta. Near the end of the war, Thomas served as one of Jefferson Davis's aides, and at war's end, the Alabama state legislature made him a general.

Before the war, Thomas had married Mary Ketchum, daughter of one of Mobile's most important families. It was their daughter, Daisy, who received the basket of flowers from the Mobile Rifle Company on Christmas Day.

Daisy inherited the house in 1911 and sold it in 1916. Over the next thirty-nine years, Oakleigh had a succession of owners and underwent a variety of renovations. In 1955, its last private owner sold the house to the city, which leased it to the Historic Mobile Preservation Society. The house is furnished with period pieces and accessories, all carefully documented and most coming from other Mobile homes. Thus, in a sense, the house is a monument to the city's famous families. The second parlor, for example, is called the Walton-LeVert Parlor because the portraits of Octavia Walton LeVert and

In the first parlor, the high ceiling accommodates the arrangement on top of the American Empire bookcase. Branches of Chinese tallow tree, pinecones and pine branches, magnolia leaves, eucalyptus, nandina, and elaeagnus make a formal spray that emphasizes Southern landscape materials.

her husband, Dr. Henry S. LeVert, hang there. The daughter of Governor George Walton of Florida, Octavia LeVert was beautiful, sophisticated, and brilliantly educated. She spoke French, Spanish, and Italian fluently, served as commissioner representing the State of Alabama at the Paris exposition in 1835, and was presented to both Queen Victoria and the Pope.

Today the house shares its three and one-half acre site with the Archives Building and an 1850 Creole cottage called the Cox-Deasy House. On the first weekend in December, candlelight bathes each decorated room at Oakleigh in a Christmassy glow, local choirs perform, and city officials preside over the lighting of the tree on the lawn. Mobile is much

Red bows with long streamers dress up the chandelier in the library. All of the furniture, paintings, and decorative objects at Oakleigh were given by Mobile families and are connected to the city's history in some way. The portrait above the mantel is of Sarah S. Evans, mother of Mobile writer Augusta Evans Wilson, the first Southern woman to earn a living with her writing. On the Empire game table is a silver tray that belonged to Octavia Walton LeVert, a nineteenth-century Mobile beauty celebrated for her intellect and social grace.

larger than it was in 1833, and the mansion that once stood outside the city is now surrounded by it. But the graceful Greek Revival structure with its winding stair reminds Mobile of the rich heritage that still shapes its character today.

Arlington

ARLINGTON, BUILT BY WILLIAM S. MUDD BETWEEN 1842 and 1850, is the only tangible evidence that there was once a pioneer community called Elyton in Jefferson County, Alabama. Incorporated in 1821, the town was the county's first permanent seat of government, but apparently it did not thrive. When General James H. Wilson led his Raiders into Alabama, he stopped at Elyton, which he described as "a poor, insignificant Southern village, surrounded by old field farms, most of which could have been bought for $5 an acre."

Although he was only in the town two hours, Wilson established headquarters at Arlington while his troops skirmished with the Confederates. Mudd, who opposed secession, gave the General the use of his office and may well have told him that Nathan Bedford Forrest had withdrawn from Tuscaloosa, leaving it undefended. Wilson sent Croxton's Brigade to capture the town. His own troops proceeded to take Selma, which was the most important munitions manufacturing center in the area.

After the war, Mudd worked to restore Alabama to the Union and to rebuild the region's economy by developing its mineral resources. In 1870, he joined nine other investors to form the Elyton Land Company, whose purpose was to establish a city at the juncture of two railroad lines being built through Jones Valley. The town, located three miles east of Elyton, was christened Birmingham in the hope that, like its English counterpart, it would become a major industrial center.

After some initial setbacks in its first decade, Birmingham began to thrive in the 1880s, and the Mudd children left Elyton for the bigger city. When Judge Mudd died in 1884, the house and its property were sold to a Birmingham entrepreneur. Then it was bought by a Midwestern real estate developer, who named the house Arlington, in honor of Robert E. Lee's home in Virginia.

The way the house looks today reflects the tastes of Robert S. Munger, who bought Arlington in 1902 as a country retreat. In the course of modernizing it, he gutted the interior, remodeled it in the Colonial Revival style, and added the second floor gallery that stretches the width of the house. In 1910, Munger moved his family there permanently. After he and his wife died, the house passed to their daughter Ruby and her husband, Alex Montgomery. Over the next thirty years, Arlington continued to be the center of family gatherings for the Munger children and grandchildren. At Christmas, an enormous juniper tree decorated with tinsel and glass balls filled one corner, and Santa distributed gifts to the youngsters gathered around.

In 1953, a coalition of citizens and the city raised the money to purchase the house, and the Arlington Historical Association restored it and furnished it with antiques. Today Arlington is Birmingham's only house museum and is the repository of one hundred years of decorative arts, displayed in room settings. The earliest piece is a Rhode Island desk, and the latest is an 1880 mirror that belonged to Robert Munger.

"Christmas at Arlington" is an annual event that until 1988 aimed to re-create "Christmas the way it used to be." That year, however, the association decided to try something entirely different and invited some of the city's best floral designers to decorate the house. Although the results do not pretend to be historically accurate, they do complement the setting and offer visitors holiday decorating ideas they can apply at home.

Over the mantel hangs a portrait of Robert Munger, who bought the house in the early 1900s and remodeled it extensively. In this room, he removed a wall to create a large parlor that would accommodate his baby grand piano. The Rococo-style chairs were given to the museum by the Bibb family, which produced two Alabama governors.

Judge Mudd used this room as an office, and it was here that he received General Wilson in March 1865. Since Arlington's opening as a house museum in the 1950s, it has been furnished with pieces donated by Alabama families. The piano on the far wall, for example, belonged to Governor Andrew Barry Moore, the state's chief executive from 1857 to 1861. In the center of the room, Empire chairs with horsehair seats are drawn up to the Empire gaming table, made in Charleston about 1820-25.

Stranahan House

SOUTH FLORIDA WAS STILL A FRONTIER WILDERNESS until the 1880s. Even in 1893 there was only one place on the road between Lake Worth and Lemon City where travelers could stop for the night. The place was the New River Overnight Camp, and in 1893 Frank Stranahan came from Ohio to run it. By the late 1890s, his trade with the Seminole Indians was thriving, and tourists from the North were beginning to discover the pleasures of Florida in winter.

Fort Lauderdale was also growing enough to need schools, and the Dade County Board of Education assigned Ivy Julie Cromartie of Lemon City (now part of Miami) to be the first teacher. She met Frank Stranahan on routine trips to the post office, and on August 16, 1900, they were married. In 1901, Frank began building a new store, a two-story block with a broad hipped roof supported on columns to create cool galleries. A large upstairs room reached by an outside stair served as a dance hall and civic center. Five years later, Frank moved the store downtown and converted this building into a

home for Ivy and himself.

Both Frank and Ivy were active in community development, Frank through business interests and Ivy through a variety of activities—she taught English, religion, and patriotism to Seminole children, headed the Women's Suffrage Association in 1916, helped start the hospital, and worked for the Audubon Society.

After Frank's suicide in 1929, Ivy rented out most of the house to tourists, but continued to live in one upstairs bedroom until her death at age ninety. Today the house is maintained as a museum, restored to depict the period from 1913 to 1915. In those years, Frank added indoor plumbing and electricity, and the couple prospered. Christmas decorations reflect a different theme each year, and each room has a tree decorated by a different store in Fort Lauderdale. Themes are dictated more by contemporary interests than historical ones, which, admittedly, would have limited appeal today: In the 1880s, Christmas in Florida often included "shooting for the beef," a backcountry tradition that involved a shooting contest, with a side of beef going to the winner. Jousts were also popular, with contestants aiming their lances at rings rather than each other. By the time Ivy and Frank were married, such contests may have declined. Their modest, comfortable home reflects Fort Lauderdale's transition from frontier outpost to bustling urban community.

The settee in the entrance hall still has its original leather seat and back. Made of American oak and carved with lions' heads, it is typical of the furniture sold through the Sears & Roebuck catalog between 1908 and 1910.

Paper fans with baby's-breath and red velvet bows ornament the tree in the bay window of the parlor. The entire house was built and paneled with now-rare Dade County pine, giving it a rustic quality that Ivy Stranahan dressed up with Victorian furnishings.

Alternating white and red bricks on the chimney breast and over the mirror reflect Frank Stranahan's late-Victorian taste for architecture decorated with contrasting colors.

Magnolia Place Inn

IN THE WEEKS BEFORE CHRISTMAS, RON STRAHAN heads for the woods with clippers and large plastic bags and collects all the juniper he can find. He brings it back to Magnolia Place Inn, where all the people on the staff, from management to housekeeping, sit on the floor and wire the branches together in long ropes. The handmade garlands are then swagged across the double verandahs of this historic Savannah inn and wrapped around the stair rail inside. Strahan also gathers hollies, pine, palm leaves, and branches of Chinese tallow tree for the arrangements that crown the front door and decorate the mantels in the guest rooms. And the staff decorates a fourteen-foot tree in the parlor.

"The tree is like a family tree," says Strahan, "because the collection of ornaments grows every year." And for many of the guests, the inn is like a family place. Relatives who are now scattered meet there for the holidays, and the small size of the inn gives it an intimate, homey feeling. In fact, guests are so pampered with personalized service and attention to the little niceties that it may be better than home. Continental breakfast is a healthy selection of fruits, pastries, croissants, and natural granola made with Georgia peaches, pecans, and other local products. Tea and wine are served in the afternoons, and a truffle and cordial at bedtime ensure sweet dreams.

Built in 1878, Magnolia Place was the home of Guerard Heyward, grandson of Thomas Heyward, a South Carolina signer of the Declaration of Independence. It represented the height of fashion, with its Victorian exuberance of architectural decoration: a mansard roof covered in octagonal tiles, scrolled brackets supporting the deep cornice, and a decorative frieze of turned spindles embellishing the double verandahs.

Gilded palmetto fans, magnolia leaves, and pinecones are combined with juniper to create a door decoration that is distinctively regional; rose and lavender ribbons, gourds, and feathers add a Victorian touch.

This room, originally the library, overlooks the park through triple-hung windows that once functioned as doors. Above the painted and marbleized slate mantel are eighteenth-century hand-colored prints by George Edwards.

A mantel constructed by carpenters on the site in the nineteenth century shows the ingenuity and design skills of local craftsmen. In this room, the prints above the mantel suggested the materials in the arrangement below: a combination of palm leaves, juniper, and Christmas fern from the Savannah landscape and carnations and exotic imports from the florist.

The verandahs overlook Forsyth Park and wrap the front and sides of the house with rounded corners that give it an expansive, welcoming graciousness. The tall windows were designed to take advantage of summer breezes. In the room that was originally the library, the windows were triple hung to serve as exits.

In 1889, Pulitzer Prize-winning poet Conrad Aiken was born in one of the bedrooms at Magnolia Place. Today each of the thirteen guest rooms is named for a hero of American or Savannah history. Each has a working fireplace and is decorated with antiques. Strahan bought the house in the late 1980s and spent a year restoring and renovating it. He and the staff have been receiving guests and dispensing Southern hospitality ever since.

Both the mantel and painted tiles are original to the house. Branches of Chinese tallow
tree and Dahoon holly create an airy triangle that fills the space below the garniture on the wall.
Juniper spills over the mantel and provides a dark green backdrop for the white carnations
and mums and gilded pinecones.

Kentucky Governor's Mansion

ON FEBRUARY 10, 1899, A FIRE LEFT THE OLD Governor's Mansion in Frankfort, Kentucky, badly damaged, giving new impetus to the move to build a new one near the recently completed Capitol Building. Securing funding from the legislature took time, however, and it was not until 1912 that the state appropriated $75,000 for the new building.

Designed by Kentucky architects C.C. and E.A. Weber of Fort Thomas, the executive residence proved to be worth the wait. Situated at the eastern edge of the Capitol grounds and overlooking the Kentucky River, the mansion recalls the Petit Trianon, Marie Antoinette's retreat at Versailles. The French Renaissance style was a direct result of the Beaux Arts influence that swept America in the 1890s and became the established architectural mode for public buildings through the 1920s. The style reflected the principles and philosophy of the École des Beaux Arts in Paris, where some of America's most important architects studied. The twenty-five room structure was completed in time for then-Governor James B. McCreary to move in on January 15, 1914. On January 20, he hosted the first official state reception, welcoming nearly one thousand guests to what the local papers described

The drawing room, sometimes called the First Lady's parlor, achieves a subtle harmony with four textures of paint in cream and palest green, champagne-colored silk window hangings, and upholstered French-made reproduction chairs, settees, and benches. The wall colors are those originally used when the mansion was built. The furnishings, produced early in this century, and the window treatments are typical of Beaux-Arts style interiors between 1890 and World War I.

Photographed during the administration of Governor Wallace Wilkinson, the grand stairway is dressed for the holidays with gold lamé bows and garlands starred with white lights. The stairs lead from the state rooms on the first floor to the First Family's private rooms on the second and third floors. The center table, which stands at the crossing of the two main halls, was made by Parisian cabinetmaker Antoine Linke early in this century.

as "one of the most palatial residences to be found anywhere."

It is indeed palatial. Standing on a knoll overlooking the Kentucky River, the mansion is built of brick faced with Kentucky limestone and crowned with a stone balustrade. Four pairs of two-story columns form a portico framing the main entrance, which opens onto a wide hall. Inside, two intersecting halls divide the first floor roughly into quarters. The two front rooms—the drawing room and the governor's reception room—are for official receptions. At the back of the house, flanking the grand stairway, are the family and state dining rooms. A one-story wing at one end of the mansion contains the sun parlor and a reception hall; at the opposite end is the grand ballroom. On the second and third floors are family and state bedrooms, studies, conference rooms, and offices.

When the mansion was finished in 1914, its exterior expressed the same neoclassical theme as the state capitol, but the interiors and the landscape were never finished in the French style. In fact, the architects' original intent was not fulfilled until nearly seventy years later.

In 1980, newly elected Governor John Y. Brown, Jr., and First Lady Phyllis George Brown moved into the mansion, only to discover that the residence needed significant architectural and cosmetic repairs. The state appropriated $2.5 million toward the project, and money came from federal revenue-sharing funds. But perhaps most significant in terms of popular support were the efforts of Save the Mansion, Inc. This organization of concerned citizens raised $1.5 million from private sources, including major corporations as well as thousands of individuals all over the state.

Dr. William Seale, noted architectural historian, professor, and author from Alexandria, Virginia, served as consultant on the restoration. With his guidance, the interiors were restored and furnished in a style consistent with the Beaux Arts architecture. Later, a formal landscape design based on French gardens was implemented.

The first floor of the mansion is open to the public for tours year-round on Tuesday and Thursday mornings. One popular time to visit is, not surprisingly, during the Kentucky Derby festivities in May. The other is at Christmas, when the state rooms are decorated. Then holiday trimmings add a festive note to interiors that are both dignified and gracious.

The sun parlor, adjoining the formal drawing room, seems a surprisingly intimate room for the first floor. It is actually a re-creation of the original sun parlor, which was across the hall and was converted in the 1940s into a coat room and lounge. Instead of the original wooden floor, however, a black and white marble one was installed as a more practical solution for the display of plants. The wicker furniture, including the still-functioning phonograph, dates to about 1910-20 and is all Kentucky made. It was collected by Phyllis George Brown, First Lady during the renovation of the mansion; she had the wicker painted blue-green and the cushions covered in chintz.

Callanwolde

In 1892 Asa G. Candler of Atlanta changed America's drinking habits by founding the Coca-Cola Company. Although his attention shifted to real estate by 1905, the soft drink and its secret formula stayed in the family until around 1915, when he sold the company for $25 million. Candler shared his good fortune immediately, giving $1 million to his brother, Bishop Warren Candler of the Methodist Episcopal Church South, to build Emory University. And he settled princely sums on his sons, Howard and Walter, who proceeded to construct huge Tudor-style homes in Druid Hills.

This vast wooded acreage northeast of Atlanta had been opened by an ambitious real estate developer in the 1890s with the goal of building an exclusive suburban neighborhood. He had even hired America's greatest landscape architect, Frederick Law Olmstead, to design the roads, parks, and house lots. But in 1908 the developer sold the property to Asa G. Candler.

Several years later, Candler gave his brother, Warren, seventy-five acres in Druid Hills for the

An enormous tree decorated by the Atlanta Chapter of the American Needlepoint Guild dominates the great hall. Above the arch, pre-cast masonry grillwork hides part of the mechanism of the organ, one of Callanwolde's unique features. Its five divisions are located over the front entrance hall, on the third floor, and over the stairwell.

The grand staircase invites grand treatment, supplied here with yards of gold lamé and fantasy topiaries made of curly willow branches wired together. Craft foam serves as a foundation for the explosion of color and texture: chrysanthemums, eucalyptus, palmetto, cock's-comb, artificial grapes, statice, preserved roses, dried hydrangea highlighted with gold spray paint, and blue Christmas balls.

The limestone fireplace in the game room is carved with medieval heraldic crests, and the walls are simulated leather. Twin arrangements of pine, magnolia leaves, lotus pods, eucalyptus, and artificial crabapples frame the bronze mantel set, *Diana of the Hunt*, ca. 1880. Baby's-breath, beeswax candles, and white bisque ornaments decorate the tree.

new university. It was apparently intended to replace Emory College, a small Methodist school in Oxford, Georgia, that Asa's son Howard had attended. Pittsburgh architect Henry Hornbostel was hired to design the campus, and in 1917 Howard Candler commissioned him to design his home, too.

Hornbostel looked to Tudor England for inspiration. The Tudor style spoke of comfortable, aristocratic antiquity, and it was one of the most popular of the academic revival styles between 1910 and 1940. Candler may also have felt that it suited his English ancestry. In 1655, his forebear William Candler had been rewarded for loyal service to Oliver Cromwell with Callan Castle in Ireland. ("Wold" is Old English for wood or forest, hence

the mansion's name.) A century later, Daniel Candler married a young Irish Catholic woman and emigrated to America, along with twenty-eight servants. After settling briefly in Virginia, the Candlers moved to Georgia and established their dynasty in the New World.

Howard Candler did not play any musical instruments, but he loved music—so much so that he had a pipe organ specially designed and installed at Callanwolde. The console was in the great hall, where the Candler children had weekly lessons with well-known Atlanta organist Dr. Charles Sheldon. The organ's five divisions (great, choir, swell, solo, and echo) were secreted in chambers over the entrance hall, the side entrance and billiard room, the main staircase, and the winter room. The sound came out through pre-cast masonry grillwork over the stone arches, and switches on the console allowed the organist to direct the music into any one or a combination of the openings. Candler's musical and social connections stretched around the globe: organist Marcel Dupré from Notre Dame Cathedral performed here, as did grand opera singer Rosa Ponselle and light opera star Irene Dunne.

When these and other illustrious guests came to Callanwolde, they found an estate that was almost a world in itself. In addition to formal gardens and a conservatory, there were vegetable gardens, fruit and nut trees, chickens, turkeys, and cows to supply a variety of fresh foodstuffs in season. A tennis court and swimming pool with clubhouse and game room provided recreation.

Callanwolde was home to Howard Candler's family for thirty-nine years. In 1959, two years after Candler's death, his wife donated the entire estate and most of its furnishings to Emory University, whose board of trustees Candler had chaired for

nearly forty years. (His brother Walter's house is now the residence of the president of the university.) In 1972 a citizens' committee raised funds to buy Callanwolde. It has been placed on the National Register of Historic Places and is now the Callanwolde Fine Arts Center.

"Christmas at Callanwolde" is one of the center's two main fund-raising events. The rooms are normally used as classrooms, so for the two weeks in December that Callanwolde is decorated for Christmas, florists and designers bring in everything they need to create their vignettes. With a different theme every year, no two Christmases are alike. The proceeds help ensure that the center can maintain its year-round offerings of visual, performing, and literary arts classes for adults and children.

Designed for a Victorian effect, the child's room features a tree hung with lavender paper bows and ornaments of natural materials. Statice, rosebuds, and artificial berries make up tiny wreaths and embellish grapevine hearts and rabbits.

Graylyn

WHEN GRAYLYN WAS COMPLETED IN 1932, IT WAS the second largest private residence in North Carolina, surpassed only by Biltmore. Although far larger than most affluent homes of the late 1920s, it exemplified the period's preference for academically correct interpretations of historical styles. But, again according to the taste of the period, the architectural language chosen for the outside did not necessarily correspond to that chosen for the inside. In fact, interiors often included a catalogue of styles. At Graylyn, the Norman Revival exterior continued inside with a medieval entrance hall, which then led to a Georgian living room, an Adamesque dining room, and a Norman stair tower. Elsewhere were a Persian card room and an Art Deco indoor swimming pool. It was like a scrapbook of the places to which the Gray family had traveled and of the art and architecture they had seen.

While it was the financial success of Bowman Gray, Sr., that underwrote construction of Graylyn, the design and decoration of the house itself was his wife's project. Nathalie Lyons Gray found the land when the couple decided to move to the country; she chose the architect, twenty-eight-year-old Luther Lashmit of Northup & O'Brien, Architects; and she knew what she wanted each room to look like. She even had a special set of blueprints made to take with her on trips to Europe so that she could purchase architectural elements as she found them.

The house, designed to recall those in Normandy and Brittany, forms an oblique L that

Nathalie Gray assembled architectural elements from around the world for the interiors of Graylyn. This carved stone doorway separating the vestibule from the entrance hall is the oldest such artifact, a fifteenth-century French door frame. A French mantel hoods the fireplace in the hall beyond; the German suit of armor dates to ca. 1580. For the annual Christmas open house, floral designer J. Potter Paul framed the doorway with magnolia leaves and bouquets of dried hydrangea fastened to a garland of silk fir. Accented with burgundy and gold drapery cords and big burgundy bows, the fresh and dried materials effectively disguise the artificial material.

stretches 240 feet. The fieldstone walls and slate roof are a picturesque shell for a technologically modern residence. A skeleton of steel and reinforced concrete made the structure sturdy and, it was incorrectly believed, fireproof. The house was completely soundproofed with concrete ceilings and walls and equipped with sophisticated air-cleaning and heating systems. It had its own telephone system, with the switchboard in the basement. A radio system in the attic sent music into all of the major living areas. Some of the bathrooms sported gold-plated fixtures while others had marble, and each bathroom on the second floor was unique. Mr. Gray's had white marble walls, with a medicine cabinet cut into one of them to keep medicine cool, and a shower with seventeen heads.

For the interiors, Nathalie Gray collected paneling, door surrounds, and mantels from Europe. When antique paneling was not available, she had reproductions made in New York City. She also commissioned new ironwork from the Philadelphia craftsman Joseph Barton Benson and selected hand-painted tiles from the Enfield Pottery and Tile Works of Pennsylvania for the pool and second-floor bathrooms.

Life at Graylyn recalled an earlier era. At a time when even affluent people were choosing smaller, more compact homes that could be run with fewer servants, the Grays built an estate that required a staff of thirty-five, including a greenhouse supervisor and a poultryman. A farm on the eighty-seven-acre estate provided most of the food for the family, house guests, and the staff. During the holidays, the poultry manager might be asked to supply sixty to ninety dozen eggs at a time. There were also bee-hives, which were moved to Roaring Gap in the summer so that the bees could make sourwood honey.

The master of this estate, Bowman Gray, Sr., was born in Winston-Salem, North Carolina, in 1874. He was the son of a founder of the Wachovia National Bank and after graduating from the University of North Carolina at Chapel Hill, he returned to the bank to start working as a teller. But in spite of the security and good pay ($1,500 a year), Bowman was dissatisfied. In 1895, he quit to become a traveling salesman for R. J. Reynolds Tobacco Company, earning $5 a week.

The challenge suited him. He helped make the company the largest of the Big Four tobacco companies, and his hard work was rewarded first with the presidency and then with chairmanship of the board. Nathalie was equally energetic, an intrepid world traveler and tireless supporter of philanthropic and community organizations. They had

Cantilevered stairs spiral up the octagonal tower. The handrail and balusters, crafted by Joseph Barton Benson of Philadelphia, are swagged with dried hydrangea, Spanish moss, pinecones, and chinaberries attached to a foundation of silk garland. The dried materials subtly echo the colors in the sixteenth-century needlepoint that covers the settee and chair, which are original to the house. (The harpsichord was brought in especially for the open house.)

Christmas even comes to the swimming pool, where a tree is decorated with white lights and pink poinsettias, both fresh and silk. The heated indoor pool was intended to recall an ocean liner pool, complete with portholes. A handcrafted iron railing by Joseph Barton Benson lines the balcony. Art Deco murals of undersea life, painted by George J. Novikoff of Baltimore, had deteriorated badly by the 1940s, but in the 1980-84 restoration, they were reproduced by Winston-Salem artist Armand deNavarre.

For the dining room, Nathalie Gray chose neoclassical Adamesque architectural details and a late eighteenth-century English marble mantel. The table is set with the family's original flatware, china, and table linens, and the Schofield (Baltimore) silver service on the side table was a gift of the Bowmans to each other for their twenty-fifth wedding anniversary. For Christmas, J. Potter Paul decorated the mantel with fresh greenery attached to a base of artificial garland.

two sons, Bowman, Jr., and Gordon. Bowman followed in his father's footsteps, starting out in the sales department of R. J. Reynolds Tobacco Company in 1930 and working his way up to chairman of the board twenty-nine years later. When the United States entered World War II, Bowman's contribution included developing intelligence techniques that are still used by the U.S. Naval Intelligence Service. Gordon also distinguished himself in the military, as junior officer on General Omar Bradley's Advanced Headquarters Staff. Appointed Secretary of the Army by President Harry Truman in 1949, he was also a state senator, a newspaper publisher, president of the University of North Carolina from 1950 to 1955, and chairman of the National Trust for Historic Preservation.

Graylyn served as a home for only fourteen years. In 1935, three years after the Grays moved in, Bowman Gray, Sr., died. Nathalie Gray continued to live in the house until she remarried in 1938, and each of her sons brought his bride there for the first years of their marriage. In 1946, the Grays donated the estate to the Bowman Gray School of Medicine of Wake Forest University, which used it as a psy-

chiatric hospital, then for classrooms. After Gordon Gray bought Graylyn back from the medical school and donated it to the university proper in 1972, it served a variety of purposes.

In 1980, fire broke out on the third floor, destroying it and leaving the first and second floors badly damaged from smoke and water. Restoration returned the mansion to its 1932 appearance, and the third floor, which originally contained walk-in storage closets, was rebuilt to incorporate additional bedrooms. Now owned by Wake Forest University, the house serves as a luxurious executive conference center for corporations, foundations, government officials, and medical meetings.

Two shades of walnut were used to panel the living room in the English Georgian style. The French nineteenth-century table between the couch and the upholstered armchairs is original to the house, as are the brocade curtains, the antique English marble mantel, and the late seventeenth-century portrait over it.

Bayou Bend

WHY JAMES STEPHEN HOGG SADDLED HIS BABY daughter with the name *Ima* is anybody's guess. Ima insisted that he named her for the heroine of a poem his brother wrote. Virginia Bernhard, author of *Ima Hogg: The Governor's Daughter*, notes that according to one rumor, the colorful, six-foot, three-hundred-pound lawyer did it just to grab voters' attention in an election year. It was a name that inevitably inspired juvenile puns such as the tale that she had a sister named Ura.

The truth is that Ima was James Hogg's only daughter and by all accounts, his darling. On her seventeenth birthday, he wrote to her, "In every feature of your face, in every movement of your hand I can see your Mother. Perhaps this of all other causes accounts for my partiality for you. . . . In you I look for a friend and counsellor as wise, as faithful, as true." She, in turn, adored him and defended his reputation against all criticism throughout her long life. And she rose above the burden of her name to become one of the most influential figures in the cultural life of Texas.

Born in 1882, Ima was eight years old when her father was elected governor of the state of Texas, and the family—which included Ima's older brother, Will, and two younger brothers, Mike and Tom—moved to the Governor's Mansion in Austin. Five years later, her mother died after a long battle with tuberculosis. For a while, an aunt moved in to supervise the children. But they were so unhappy

that Governor Hogg sent the three youngest to a nearby boarding school until his term ended the next year.

Ima had played the piano since she was three, and at the turn of the century, after two years at the University of Texas, she went to New York to study piano. Her father's death in 1906 left her devastated, and music proved to be her therapy. At her brother Will's urging, she went to Germany for two years to study. Sometime during that period she decided not to pursue a career as a concert pianist, but for about ten years after returning to Houston she taught piano to a small group of students, some of whom did become professionals. In 1913, Ima also initiated efforts to start a symphony in Houston, persuading a friend who was a cellist to round up enough other musicians to offer a concert. From that modest beginning, the symphony and its group of supporters grew. Miss Hogg served twelve terms as president of the Houston Symphony Society, managed the fund-raising campaigns, and worked, with great diplomacy, to make sure the symphony's artistic and financial leadership were the best available.

In 1919, oil was discovered on the family land, and overnight the Hoggs were independently wealthy. Will was deeply involved in real estate development as well as philanthropy and community improvement. According to Virginia Bernhard, it is largely as a result of his efforts that Houston has a downtown civic center, a spacious municipal park, and one of the most beautiful suburban communities in the country, River Oaks.

Paneled walls repeat the curving crests of the William and Mary banister-back side chairs, which were made in New England between 1700 and 1725. In the center is an eighteenth-century child's chair, also from New England. The portrait *Boy in Brown* is attributed to an anonymous artist known as the Pierpont Limner, active between 1711 and 1716. The checkerboard-painted oak floor is based on a floor treatment in a colonial house in Hopkinton, New Hampshire.

Pine and baby's-breath form a cloud of green and white across the marble fireplace, embellished with ormolu ornaments. The orange and green of citrus complement the black basalt Wedgwood and the bronze lamps, which were made in New York ca. 1825-35, probably by Baldwin Gardiner. Above, the room is reflected in the curving surface of the Federal girandole mirror.

Begun in 1924, River Oaks was developed along the lines of exclusive country-club neighborhoods cropping up all over the country. Like these, River Oaks featured large lots, winding roads, and restrictive covenants on the size, kind, and siting of houses that could be built there. John Staub, a young New York architect, was one of three who designed a number of houses on speculation for the development. Will asked Ima to consult with Staub on designs for some of them, and in 1927 she asked him to design a house for her two unmarried brothers and her.

The house was a collaborative effort, built on the largest lot in the development. Miss Ima, now forty-five years old, had traveled extensively and had definite ideas about the kind of house best suited to Houston's climate. The architecture of New Orleans, combined with the pale pink stucco of Greece, resulted in a mansion that Staub dubbed Latin Colonial—Georgian in its massing and symmetry, Spanish Colonial in its painted stucco exterior and wrought iron trim. To achieve the pink color, crushed minerals were mixed with the wet cement. The sashes and blinds were painted brown and then glazed pale green so that they would harmonize with the copper roof as it weathered.

In 1920, Ima had begun studying and collecting American art and furniture, and by 1927 she had accumulated an impressive collection of Early American pieces. To create appropriate settings for them, handhewn floor planks, woodwork, and a mantel were brought from old houses on the East Coast. Other paneling and mantels were handcrafted to reproduce antique models.

Although the house was built for Will, Ima, and Mike, only Ima really made her home there. Mike married in 1929 and built a house next door. Will was in Europe and South America for much of 1928 and 1929 and died in 1930. So for the next thirty-five years, Ima lived at Bayou Bend, working tirelessly on cultural and civic projects and adding to her collection of American decorative arts. Ultimately, she amassed a body of work that is second only to the trove at Winterthur in Delaware.

The Empire center table, made in Philadelphia ca. 1825-35, is set for coffee and tea. Its top can be turned to a vertical position to show off the ebonized, stenciled, and veneered surface. The shape of the London-made harp is repeated in the back of the New York-made chair, which is one of only a few known to exist. The gilt bronze chandelier, made in France in the early nineteenth century, is hung with pine, nandina berries, baby's-breath, and copper ribbon.

A tree of apples and boxwood stands on the walnut drop-leaf table, which was made in Maryland or Virginia between 1710 and 1725. The chair on the left was made in England, 1690-1705, and imported to Boston. It bears a brass plaque on the back listing its various Boston owners. On the right, a Boston-made chair represents the transition from the William and Mary style to the Queen Anne. The New England joint stool on the near side of the table represents the most common type of seating in the seventeenth and early eighteenth centuries. Over the fireplace hang mezzotint portraits of William and Mary.

A visit to that estate gave Miss Ima the idea of turning her home into a museum, and in 1958 she began the process of converting it into a facility that could be opened to the public. In 1966, Bayou Bend opened as a wing of the Museum of Fine Arts, Houston. Furnishings on display now include examples by or attributed to some of the most important American furniture makers, including John Townsend, Duncan Phyfe, and John Henry Belter. Portraits by John Singleton Copley, Charles Willson Peale, and Gilbert Stuart hang on the walls. Following Miss Ima's wishes, the Bayou Bend Advisory Committee and the museum's Board of Trustees continue to acquire works that exemplify the very best of early American decorative arts.

In a photo taken at the turn of the century, Miss Ima, as she came to be known in Texas, looks sweet and dreamy, a petite young woman with an incredibly tiny waist, sparkling eyes, and light blonde hair piled softly on top of her head in the manner of a Gibson girl. But that gentle exterior belied a complex and forceful personality. Her powers of persuasion became legendary, and she used them not only to organize the Houston Symphony and create a museum of decorative arts but also to initiate music and art education programs in the public schools, to establish the Hogg Foundation for Mental Health at the University of Texas and the Child Guidance Center of Houston, to protect Memorial Park from commercial development, and to promote historic preservation in Texas. The uninitiated may smirk at the mention of Ima Hogg's name, but for Texans, it is the name of the patron saint of culture.

In 1850, Thomas Flintoff painted this portrait of the children of Judge William Jefferson Jones and his wife, Elizabeth Giberson Jones. The family had just moved to Galveston, Texas, from Columbus, Ohio. One son, Walter, became mayor of Galveston in 1899. The one-drawer chest with geometric panels was made in Massachusetts in the seventeenth century.

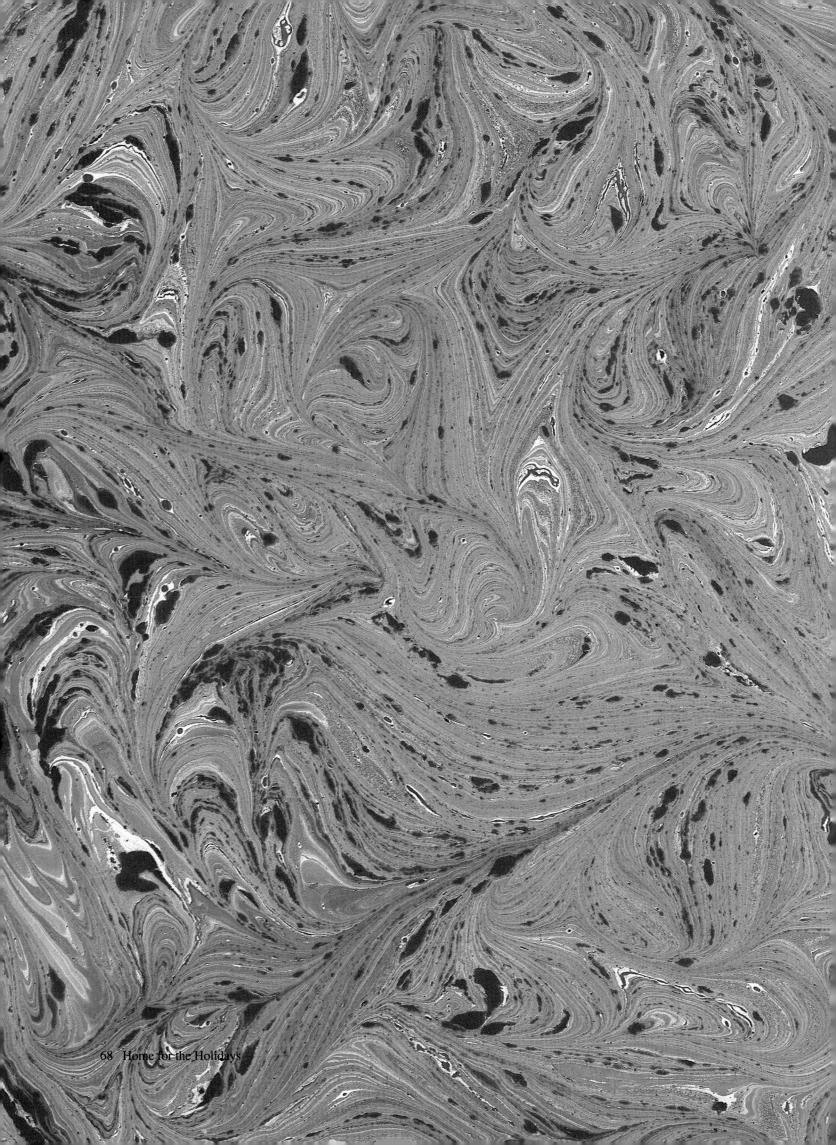

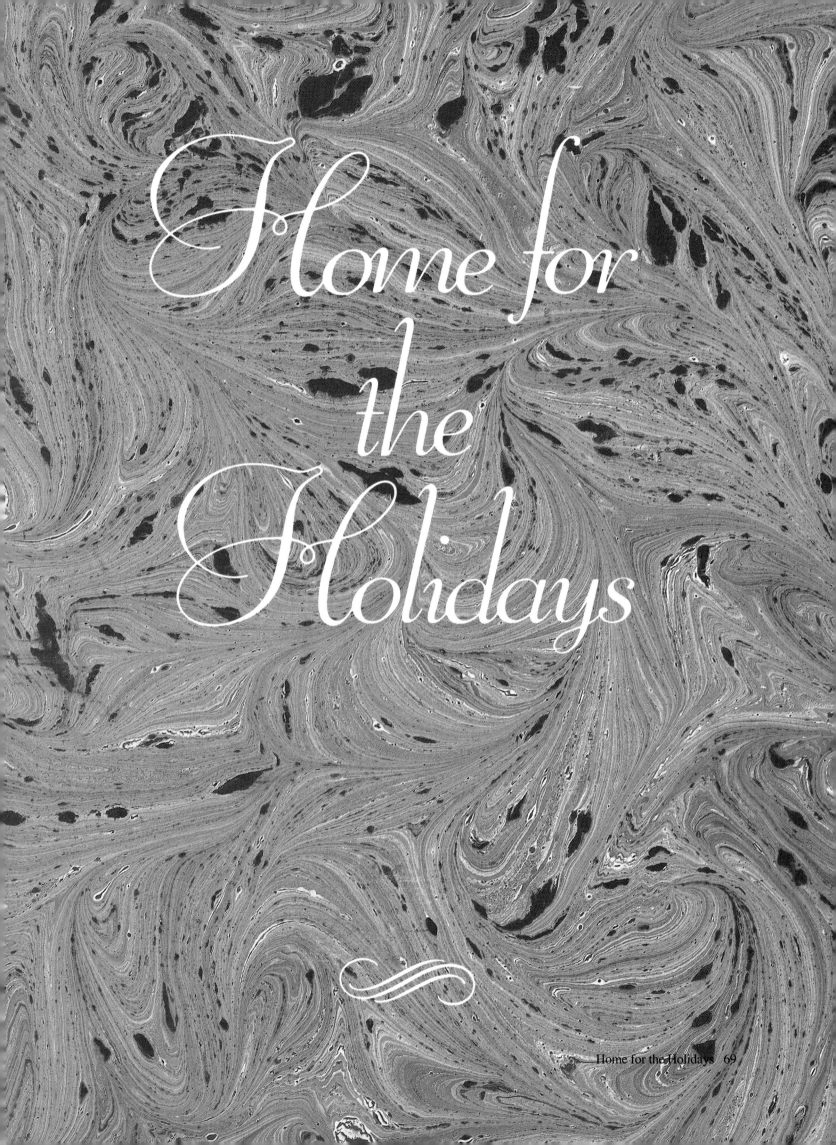

Home for the Holidays

Folk Art Focus

SANTAS ON THE STAIRS, SANTAS IN THE HALL, Santas in the desk, and on the cupboard shelves. Everywhere you look in Nancy and Dick Gould's house, there are Santas. Only one or two recall the jolly old elf made famous by the Coca-Cola ads; most are folk art or antique interpretations of St. Nicholas in his various international and legendary manifestations.

Collecting the folk art Santas became an absorbing passion, and, as often happens with collectors who are also entrepreneurs, the Santas—and the artists who created them—found their way to Nancy's shop, Eldred Wheeler, in Houston. The one-of-a-kind figures proved so popular that she now carries what may be the best collection of handcrafted Santas in the country.

The shop itself developed out of Nancy's own search for early American antiques. She and Dick bought a New England Colonial-style house more than ten years ago, and she was determined to furnish it with period pieces.

Inside the pigeonholes of a Connecticut slant-lid cherry desk from about 1750-80 are Santas old and new. On the desk top is a Pennsylvania grain-painted hetchel, a tool for combing wool. Florida berries are arranged in its pronged, froglike center section, which originally combed the wool. On the desk is a bound manuscript entitled *The Elements of Navigation*, written in 1804 by Francis Wilson Ellis at age thirteen, while he was at the Royal Naval College in England.

Wooden and chalkware Santas climb the stairs beneath a swag of Noble fir, nandina, and black ribbon. On the paint-decorated blanket chest, which is signed by Johannes Rank of Pennsylvania, is a St. Nicholas by Norma De Camp.

Rod-back Windsor chairs from about 1810 are pulled up to the shoe-foot chair table, ca. 1740, from New York. A wreath rings the period American hurricane lamp, which was filled with cranberries after the candles were put in place. Behind the sofa, a maple chest-on-chest bears the inscription of its original owner, J. Frederick, Wells, Maine. On top is a bride's box, ca. 1850. The banister-back armchair and child's ladder-back rocker are ca. 1760.

Over the mantel, a primitive oil painting titled *What Cheer* depicts Pilgrims meeting Native Americans. The Santa in his polar bear-drawn sleigh was carved by craftsman Lou Schifferl.

She laughs now as she recalls her naïveté; she soon found that the best early American furniture was in the museums, and what was available was not affordable. "So I started looking for well-made reproductions, built by traditional methods and with old tools," she says. That led her to search for other types of craftspeople; now her shop carries the work of some 550 artisans.

Talking to her about the handmade objects and antiques with which she is surrounded is like opening a decorative-arts encyclopedia. She can tell you not only the date and provenance of each item, but also its purpose, method, or history. The tin pipe tray on her dining table, for example, replicates the kind used in taverns and inns. Clay pipes rested on the rack, and tobacco was kept in an "honor box" on the bottom tray. Tavern patrons might borrow a pipe, have a smoke, then break off the tip and place the pipe back on the rack for its next user.

A pipe tray by tinsmith Jerry Martin holds fruit and greenery instead of the clay pipes that such trays originally held. Another Lou Schifferl Santa, this one riding a reindeer, is on the window seat.

Contemporary and antique redware and handcrafted Santas
fill the shelves of a Pennsylvania pewter cupboard made by
cabinetmaker Steven Van Ormer.

Inside a child's grain-painted doll trunk from the mid-
nineteenth century are pysanky- and scratch-decorated eggs
by contemporary craftswomen. Rare brass hog scraper
candlesticks and chalkware deer from the nineteenth century
stand on either side of the box.

74 Home for the Holidays

Flanking the Pennsylvania blanket chest, which dates to the early nineteenth century, are banister-back armchairs by contemporary craftsman Allen Breed. On the chest stand three magnificent Christmas figures: Ghost of Christmas Past and Blue Father Christmas by Denise Calla and Sitting Santa by Norma De Camp. Above them hangs a painting, *Boy with Spaniel*, attributed to Joseph Whiting Stock, 1815-55.

There are also pysanky- and scratch-decorated eggs. Pysanky is the wax-resist and dye technique associated with Ukrainian eggs, but it was also practiced in Czechoslovakia and Germany. "Eggs were a popular gift for various occasions," Nancy explains, "because everyone had chickens. How you decorated it depended on the occasion—wedding, birth, anniversary, or Christmas. It can take up to fourteen hours to do one egg." Scratch-decoration is a Pennsylvania German technique for embellishing Easter eggs. The eggs are dipped in dyes made with onion skins, red cabbage, or other natural materials that yield soft colors. The design is then scratched into the surface of the shell. Nancy points out that while some people remove the egg white and yolk before decorating the shell, others simply boil the eggs first. "If the shell isn't cracked, the white will eventually evaporate and the yolk will get hard like a rubber ball."

In November and December, all of the art and artifacts in Nancy's shop relate to the season, and Eldred Wheeler turns into a Christmas village packed with unique handcrafted ornaments and decorations.

"Every square inch has Christmas things in it or on it—it *is* overwhelming," admits Nancy. In July, she and her assistants repeat the season with real trees, fresh greens, and unconventional decorations such as red peppers, fruits and vegetables, American flags, and stars.

"We just love Christmas," says Nancy. Far from draining her enthusiasm for decorating at home, the November-December preparations at work just seem to whet her appetite for more. "We go home and do the whole thing all over," she says. "I grew up that way, with Christmas being the focal point of the year for my family. My mother would fill the whole house. You couldn't walk into the living room for all the packages spread out on the floor."

Dick, who has his own business, is the antiques expert of the pair, says Nancy. For herself, she claims no special background or training for what she does—"just a love for it and a love for learning about it." Her enthusiasm is contagious and her energy boundless, especially when it comes to the holidays. It is difficult to imagine coming away from her home—or her shop—without a hefty dose of Christmas spirit.

Sophisticated Celebration

DAVID STONE'S HOLIDAY DECORATIONS ARE definitely unconventional. In one sense, they are so subtle you might not realize he has done anything seasonal at all; in another, they are so flamboyant that only a major celebration could account for them. To this Houston interior designer, "cute Christmas" is anathema. Then David laughs and admits he must be mellowing, because he thinks cuteness is "okay for people with kids. But adults need a

Charles X chairs sit on either side of a Biedermeier chest where Wedgwood basalt pieces from the King Tut commemorative collection are displayed. A footed marble dish holds bright red pears and fat blueberries in a subtle nod to the season.

Solar-gray mirrored walls and gleaming wood floors make a sleek backdrop for holiday decorating: red-flowered chintz slipcovers, a table skirted in silver moiré and red leather, and spectacular arrangements and wreath by Bobb Wirfel. The painting behind the love seat is by Eugene Bavinger.

The English Regency commemorative clock honoring the Duke of Wellington always stands on the mantel, flanked by Italian alabaster cannons and Charles X candlesticks. For Christmas, a diamond-shaped wreath hangs above the clock.

more sophisticated look for Christmas." In exemplary fashion, he avoids the traditional in favor of a more urbane approach and restricts his decorating to the rooms where guests will be.

In the foyer, a red-and-white drapery cord swags across the nineteenth-century Austrian mirror, and bright red pears and blueberries fill a marble dish as the only concessions to the season. In the living room, red-flowered chintz frames the doorway and dresses the sofas especially for Christmas. David also moves a round table into the center of the room and skirts it with silver moiré and red

Instead of a tree, David has a massive double arrangement. The urns are mid-nineteenth century, patinized and gilded bronze on black-and-rouge-royale marble bases. The arrangements, designed to work as a single composition, combine fresh, dried, and artificial elements for an extravagantly baroque effect. The materials include amaryllis, eucalyptus seedpods, deodar cedar, smilax berries, bayberry, sycamore balls, apples, and gold-sprayed leaves and pinecones.

leather; the exuberant double arrangement of amaryllis, berries, fruit, and deodar cedar serves as his tree. Even the wreath over the fireplace is unconventional, a diamond shape studded with a long list of dried and natural materials. Rosebuds, juniper, Florida berries, holly berries, bayberry, spruce, Chinese tallow tree, dried cock's-comb, and gold-sprayed pinecones are arranged in bands around the shape so that the colors shade from deep red to peach to yellow and gold. David has worked with florist Bobb Wirfel for years and Wirfel knows Stone's tastes. "I tell him what china I'm going to use and where I want decorations, and he puts them together," says David.

His holiday entertaining usually consists of Sunday brunches for twenty-five to thirty people or a combination of dinners and brunches. In the dining room, arrangements of gray-green succulents enhance his quirky collection of nineteenth-century nickel-plated bronze candlesticks and harmonize with the walls, covered in Fortuny fabric. The candlesticks are classic English and French decorative pieces, he says. Each has a tripod base with animal feet and a creature climbing up the shaft—realistically rendered lizards, rats, beetles, snakes, even alligators. David says he had them nickel plated to add some sparkle in the dining room, which is very dark. In the alcove above the faux-tortoise cabinets, amaryllis and river stones play off the painting by Bill Shepherd.

David may describe himself jokingly as coming from the "bah-humbug" school of Christmas. But anyone who creates such a sumptuous setting for entertaining friends is certainly no Scrooge.

For holiday entertaining, David usually serves buffet-style Sunday brunch. When he opts for a seated dinner, guests take their places in Biedermeier Revival chairs, ca. 1900, around the dining table, which is set with Ricci silver plate and Waterford crystal.

An arrangement of bromeliads, succulents, bayberry, and various types of silvery foliage fills the nickel-plated bronze urn, which dates to about 1830. The candlesticks, collected over a period of twenty years, feature a menagerie of creepy-crawlies and were crafted in the early 1800s, in the English Regency and French Empire periods.

Curling Ribbon and Candles

ORDINARILY, P. J. MARSHALL DECORATES FOR Christmas right after Thanksgiving. That way everything is ready for her son's early-December birthday and the succession of open houses that she and her husband, Marv, host for all their friends. But the year our photographer showed up, the Marshalls were doing some remodeling, and the normal routine was in disarray.

"I usually like to do the decorating myself," says P. J., "but I have my own business, plus two little children, so I decided that the only way to keep my sanity was to have someone else do it." As it happened, Michele Bray was launching just such a service. "She sent out a card that looked like an invitation, listing what she would do," recalls P. J. "It sounded great, so I called her." P. J. and Michele talked about the family's likes and dislikes and the kind of look P. J. wanted: sophisticated yet fun for the children. Michele suggested adding brass horns and curling ribbon to the usual greenery and fruit. The Marshalls liked the effect so much that now they repeat it every year.

Another innovation was a special tree for the children. Once the ornaments were divided, however, there weren't quite enough to fill both trees. The solution: They brought daughter Taylor's

P. J. Marshall chose burgundy and hunter green over brighter Christmas colors because the effect is more formal and the combination blends better with the color of her door and entry hall. Tiny white lights and velvet ribbons were spiraled around the garland before it was hung; then pinecones and artificial cherries were wired in place. The wreath is made from a commercially available mixture of fresh cedar, fir, and juniper wired to strong cable and sold in one-hundred-yard rolls. Decorator Michele Bray cut the rope to the desired length and attached it to a frame, then wired embellishments in place (a hunting horn, cinnamon sticks, Florida berries, pinecones, and bow) for a quick custom-designed wreath.

Madame Alexander dolls down from the shelf and positioned them carefully on the branches. Because the dolls were gifts to Taylor from family and godparents, displaying them on the tree inevitably evokes memories for everyone.

If the decorations are geared to the children's enjoyment, other traditions are also guaranteed to make their Christmases unforgettable. On Christmas Eve, family and friends gather at the Marshalls' home for a big dinner, and each person opens one gift before all go to Mass. But here's the best part: On Christmas morning, Santa himself (usually a godparent) wakes the children and takes them downstairs, where he distributes wonderful goodies from his sack.

The plump wreath propped against the mirror in this entry was originally an ordinary pinecone wreath with artificial pears glued to it. Decorator Michele Bray sprigged it with fresh fir to soften it, tucked in some artificial cherries and kumquats, and wired two horns in place. It rests on a blanket of fresh fir branches and magnolia leaves, with pinecones and branches of Florida berries placed on the fir to add texture and color. (The console itself is the decorative crest of an armoire, turned upside down and attached to a tabletop constructed to match.)

Miniature Christmas trees frame a collection of candles. The trees were made by gluing pinecones to a craft foam base. Artificial fruits and leaves, brass horns, and velvet bows were then attached with florists' picks.

Brass candlesticks of varying heights hold in place the doubled rope of artificial garland that forms the basis for this lavish mantel decoration. Artificial grapes are wired to the candlesticks to hold the grapes at the mantel's edge, and Florida berries, pinecones, and artificial fruit are tucked into the garland. Pineapples and magnolia leaves visually anchor the arrangements at each end of the mantel, and pink and orange curling ribbons and an unwound grapevine wreath add gestural, free-form lines. Taylor Marshall's collection of Madame Alexander dolls helped fill out the decorations on this, the children's, tree. It was a spur-of-the-moment inspiration that gave a personal character to the tree—and started a new tradition.

A Collector's Christmas

"CHRISTMAS IS MY FAVORITE TIME OF YEAR," SAYS
Charles Faudree, a Tulsa, Oklahoma, interior designer. His decorations go up on Thanksgiving Day
because, he explains, "I'm in the retail business and
if I don't do it then, things get too busy and I don't
feel like it." The decorations stay up through the traditional twelve days of Christmas—and sometimes
even longer. One year, out-of-town friends were
making a special trip to see his house, so he left the
decorations up until February. "They almost got the
nets after me," he jokes.

Charles used to have three trees every year: one
in the kitchen, one in the dining room, and one in
the living room. But when he moved into this New
England saltbox, he scaled it back to two.

This area adjoins the kitchen so that Charles Faudree can
enjoy his guests and cook at the same time. At Christmas, he
swags the mantel with blue spruce and hangs a spruce wreath
over the deer antlers to match the ornament-laden tree in
the corner.

The tree in the front living room is decorated with real candles, antique peach satin ribbon, gold tassels, dried roses, and pomanders. Charles's touch is light in this room and the back living and dining areas, in keeping with the colonial interiors. If these rooms look remarkably authentic, it's because they are. The original owners, Beulah Larson and her husband, scoured New England in the 1950s, gathering eighteenth-century building materials. These Oklahoma natives had fallen in love with New England antiquities and over the years had assembled a houseful of early American furniture for which they wanted an appropriate setting. They designed the house itself after the Michael Griswold house, built in 1730 in Wethersfield, Connecticut.

The stairway, flooring, paneling, exterior clapboard, all doors, window glass, and even the hardware and nails are antique. To discover the original colors for the interior woodwork, the Larsons removed layers of paint to get back to the wood. When new beading was required, it was planed by hand with antique tools.

When Charles Faudree acquired the house, his only complaint was that the kitchen was too small. He knew from previous houses he had lived in that he wanted a kitchen large enough to include a comfortable seating area so that he didn't have to leave his guests every time something needed stirring. The solution he reached with architect John Brooks

When it comes to the holidays, Charles believes in lavish feasts. The eighteenth-century Welsh dresser displays his collection of rare white Staffordshire cows.

Walton preserved the integrity of the home's original design while expanding living space generously. The garage was converted into a kitchen and great room with a cathedral ceiling, and a master bedroom and bath, breezeway, and new garage were added.

In the new great room, Charles emphasizes the season with more elaborate decorations than in the older part of the house: a tall blue spruce, greenery over the fireplace, and Christmas collectibles on display. The tree recalls those the designer remembers from his childhood, with twinkling lights, tinsel ropes, and hundreds of ornaments. Many of the ornaments are those he grew up with, and to that collection he has added Victorian ones found over the years on trips to Europe.

Another tradition from childhood that continues to be central to his celebration is Christmas morning brunch. "We always had a big country-style breakfast, with champagne, fried quail, biscuits, and gravy," Charles says. Now, he and his sister, also a Tulsa interior designer, take turns hosting it for family and friends. It's a wonderfully festive way to observe this special day.

A slender artificial tree fits into the corner of the front living room, and a garland of fresh boxwood, dried chinaberries, ribbon, and pinecones crowns the painting over the mantel. The secretary dates to the nineteenth century.

An opulent garland frames a portrait, whose subject Charles Faudree jokingly refers to as "my instant ancestor, Uncle Albert." Artificial and real greenery are wired together to make the rope that simply rests on the picture frame, along with antique drapery tassels, prizes from a Parisian flea market. Balls, pinecones, and bare branches are then tucked into the rope of greenery.

A collection of tortoiseshell boxes includes everything from ink wells and card cases to cigar boxes, tea boxes, and scent-bottle holders. Staffordshire pugs line up under a Victorian dog painting. The clock is nineteenth-century French.

Apricot-colored Staffordshire castles line up on the mantel year-round, but at Christmas trees and snow are added for a holiday look. The room is a showcase for a collection of English nineteenth-century animal paintings, a product of the Victorians' love of pets.

A Life-size Christmas Card

LIKE HER BROTHER, CHARLES, FRANCIE FAUDREE IS a collector. Canton and Imari porcelain, antique needlepoint, and Staffordshire dogs and cows fill shelves, walls, and tabletops throughout her Tulsa, Oklahoma, home. And at Christmas, she becomes a collector of people—"waifs and strays," her brother says. Christmas is a festive occasion that needs to be shared, and because the family is small, they like to bring in as many friends as they can.

Francie works with Charles at his antiques shop, and Charles served as advisor when Francie and her husband, Dale Gillman, began redecorating their home, a French Normandy-style house. Although Dale and Francie each have very definite—and independent—tastes, Charles once told a writer that the three of them "think so much alike, it's uncanny. We all like combinations of French and English furnishings. And we have the same tastes in accessories. I started Francie collecting Staffordshire when she was still too young to spell the word."

Fabrics and colors for each room were chosen to enhance the collections that would be displayed there. In the club room, for example, painted and glazed red walls give the effect of leather. Framed by golden woodwork, the walls provide a rich backdrop for Victorian paintings of dogs.

At Christmas, an enormous tree fills one corner of the club room. Topped by a Santa figure and draped with ropes of beads, the tree is encrusted with Victorian ornaments and old-fashioned icicles and looks like a Christmas card come to life. The ornaments, says Francie, are as old as she is, "and that could be considered antique." When she's told that Charles made the same quip about his tree, she laughs, admitting that people sometimes think they're twins because of that mental affinity. The tree goes up the day after Thanksgiving, Francie says, and she and Dale have at least one party before Christmas Eve, when Francie's "waifs and strays" gather to eat dinner and open presents. When it comes to celebrating the holidays, Francie, her husband, and her brother are all of one mind: the more the merrier.

A trompe l'oeil wallpaper from Brunschwig & Fils makes a dramatic backdrop for a Christmassy, snow-covered still life in the entry. A Victorian concrete garden ornament seems to bring the flowers in the nineteenth-century half-round painting out onto the table. Artificial and real fruits rest on a bed of fir and pine, and a rope of dyed, dried millet picks up the pinks in the painting.

A magnificent tree laden with glittering icicles and Victorian ornaments fills one corner of the club room. The fireplace provides the focal point at the opposite end of the room. A portrait of an English soldier is elaborately framed with a rope of artificial and fresh greenery, feathers, pomegranates, hunting horns, violins, and antique passementerie from Paris. Craft foam wired to the artificial garland provides a foundation for the feathers, pomegranates, and fresh greenery. The instruments, which are flea market finds, are carefully secured with wire to tiny tacks in the paneling.

Forced narcissus and pots of African violets are arranged in a footed silver serving dish to create a tabletop landscape for the dining room. Francie's collection of Chinese Imari is displayed on the hutch and walls.

In the library, a Napoleonic theme is carried out in prints, small busts, and hats, as well as old epaulets found on trips to England and France. An impressive pair of epaulets and a French tricornered hat embellish the wreath.

The formal elegance of the living room is enhanced with decorations that focus on the fireplace. A blanket of greenery, silk roses, pink beads, and dyed millet rest on the picture frame. The same materials are repeated on the mantel, and millet roping and beads wrap the artificial Christmas tree-shaped topiary nearby.

Decorating with Memories

A red cedar with decorations collected over several generations fills one wall in this comfortable living room, and a garland frames the portrait over the mantel.

LIVING IN THE FIRST HOUSE BUILT ON MILLEDGE Avenue in Athens, Georgia, focuses attention on history for Peggy and Denny Galis. "The house was built in 1840, and then in 1890, it was pulled by mules to this little side street," explains Peggy.

Owning one of the oldest homes in town is not the only strong tie the Galises have with local history. They have filled the interiors of the house with bits of the past. Among the most beautiful reminders of the area's heritage are the twelve antique lithographs of Indians that adorn the living room and dining room walls. "They are of the three tribes once found in Georgia—Cherokee, Creek, and Seminole," says Peggy.

Family history is kept alive through furniture and portraits, such as the primitive painting of Peggy's great-great-great-grandfather, Stephen Heard. During the American Revolution, Heard was imprisoned by the British. On the day before his scheduled execution, his nanny, Mammy Cate, visited him in jail with a big laundry basket of fresh linens on her head, saying she didn't want him to die in dirty clothing. Heard, who was of especially small stature, climbed into the basket, and Mammy Cate walked out, carrying him atop her head. Heard later became governor of Georgia.

Being surrounded by so much history makes tradition-keeping easy. "We strive to repeat customs that have been done by our families for years," says Peggy. "We always do the same thing first. The children get out an olivewood crèche, a gift from their grandmother, and we set that up to emphasize the real meaning of Christmas. Then we're ready to decorate."

The Galises favor the old-fashioned look of native cedar Christmas trees, so an enormous one fills a living room wall. "We have always handed down tree decorations in our family, including an old collection of Gorham snowflakes," explains Peggy. But by far the majority of the ornaments are handmade, including things the Galises' children have made in school over the years. Peggy hangs the children's baby silver—cups, rattles, and teething rings—on the tree as well. It's a nostalgic custom that perfectly expresses this family's memory-filled celebration.

Built in 1840, the Galises' home recalls farmhouses constructed throughout the Southeast in the nineteenth century. The tapered columns are a refinement that reveals the influence of the Greek Revival style.

Shutters flanking the door, right, look like tall packages wrapped with ribbon and decorated with "bows" of greenery.

In the dining room, an old-fashioned apple pyramid and greenery are in keeping with the house's character. On the left is a primitive portrait of Stephen Heard, a former governor of Georgia and an ancestor of Peggy's.

Simple Pleasures

CHRISTMAS COMES EARLY AND STAYS LATE AT Margaret and Merrill Sexton's Lookout Mountain, Tennessee, home. "We start decorating in early December, make a family outing to get the trees, and enjoy Christmas until after New Year's," says Margaret, an interior designer. "But I like to think that, in a way, our house shows hospitality all year long. Merrill and I want adults and children to feel the warmth and love our house extends to people of all ages, particularly at Christmas."

Their two-story stone-and-wood house, designed by local architect Klaus Nentwig, AIA, provides the Sextons with a perfect backdrop for this hospitality. During the holiday season, the friendly welcome begins at the front door. Here, Margaret hangs a large hemlock-and-holly wreath and fills the center with lemons. Greenery and red taffeta bows brighten the brass lamps that flank the door. "I like natural things for Christmas—real greenery and fruit when possible," she says.

Inside, the holiday mood continues in the festively decorated foyer. A plaid taffeta ribbon loosely wraps the garland that hangs in swags from the stair handrail. An arrangement of fruit and pinecones tops the newel post. Margaret introduces more greenery with pine boughs above the overdoors from the foyer to the living and dining rooms. And she drapes an evergreen swag around the formal portrait above the living room mantel.

A garland wrapped with plaid ribbon swags the staircase, leading the eye upward from the bouquet of fruit and pinecones on the newel post.

Folding doors in the foyer open to reveal the living room dressed for the holidays. A pine garland arranged on the overdoor sets the mood for the adjoining room.

A handmade garland of cinnamon sticks, raffia, and yarrow foliage decorates the brick fireplace. The rocking horse and oxen are from the owners' collection of antique toys.

A colorful Della Robbia garland of mixed fruits and greenery hangs over the fireplace surround. Tall red candles, an Italian Nativity scene mixed with magnolia leaves on the mantel, and a tiny Christmas tree with doll-sized ornaments and packages contribute to the room's rich ambience.

In the more rustic sitting room, Margaret designed a garland of cinnamon sticks, yarrow foliage, and strawlike raffia for the brick fireplace. Here, the collection of nutcrackers on the mantel and antique toys, including a large rocking horse and a pair of oxen pulling a wagon, underscore the old-fashioned feeling of the house. Reusing these toys and ornaments year after year has become a family tradition for the Sextons.

But most special of all is one of the simplest decorations. Copying an early American design, Margaret made a wooden gingerbread tree. "It's a family ritual for the children and me to bake the gingerbread men and hang them from the little tree," she explains. "They look forward to it every year, particularly eating the extra cookies. Christmas is my favorite time of year, and family and children are what Christmas is all about."

Doll-sized ornaments and packages decorate this miniature tree. Antique books and tiny glass balls complete the tabletop arrangement.

Italian Nativity pieces and magnolia leaves flank an antique English tortoiseshell box filled with glass balls.

A Flair for Naturals

THE CHRISTMAS TREE AT INTERIOR DESIGNER Kathleen Riley Sharman's house is usually covered with homemade ornaments, a collection of those her children have made, combined with "years of ornament exchanges" with friends. But the year these photographs were taken, Kathleen had volunteered her home for the Kappa Kappa Gamma Houston Christmas Pilgrimage. This event, which occurs every two years, is the sorority's main fund-raising activity to benefit local nonprofit rehabilitation programs. Members of the alumni association offer their homes, and the association takes it from there, appointing house chairmen and selecting some of Houston's best florists to do the decorations.

Florist Jeff Bradley developed the decorations for the Sharmans' home. "He came about a year ahead and thought about what he wanted to do," says Kathleen. "He could see it in his mind's eye, and so could I to some extent. We both have a good eye for color. So I gave him carte blanche."

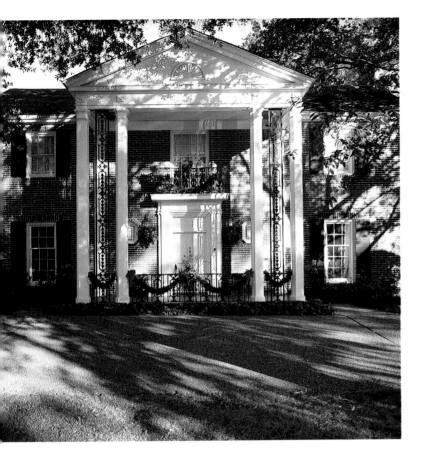

Thick ropes of English boxwood, caught up with red velvet bows, swag the porch and balcony railings. Instead of a wreath on the door, the designer created the illusion of a wreath on the railing with long branches of possum haw, beautyberry, and other branches, all anchored in a block of florists' foam.

A trio of ornamental pineapples creates a rosette above sprays of juniper, boxwood, and camellia foliage. Also built up on a foundation of florists' foam, the arrangement incorporates berried branches, red and green apples, lady apples, and piñon cones. Rubbing the apples with vegetable oil gives them a high shine and will not harm any birds that might be attracted to the fruit.

One of a pair of eighteenth-century Italian polychromed cherubs raises its hand in salutation from a throne of greenery, fruit, and flowers.

His goal, Jeff says, was "an unstructured elegance with a naturalistic flair" that would suit the formal exterior and comfortable interiors of the Sharman home. To achieve it, he combined fruit with evergreens and branches from the garden and woods, a palette of materials that works both indoors and out. Accents and variations acknowledge specific color schemes inside.

The scale of the two-story house required an oversized treatment on the wrought iron rail that encloses the porch. Thick ropes of English boxwood swag the railing at ground level and on the balcony, and a large central arrangement focuses attention on the door beyond. Another lavish bouquet serves as a flourish at the end of the stair rail.

Boxwood roping reappears in the living and dining rooms. In the latter, the roping is wound

Warm pink walls, a Sarouk carpet, and a Bailey & Griffin floral print give the living room a springtime feeling all year. Decorations emphasize the color scheme with fresh flowers and ornamental pineapples. Green apples, lady apples, and a pomegranate, cut in half to reveal the pattern of its shiny seeds, complete the design.

Home for the Holidays   107

Simplicity is the best companion for the delicate intricacy of this rare Adam sconce, one of a pair that hangs in the entry hall. A glazed saucer filled with craft foam and covered with sphagnum moss provides the foundation for pears and lady apples secured with florists' picks. Pepper berries complement the yellow-green fruit, and narcissus sprout from a small liner wedged into the top of the craft foam, which is stacked like a wedding cake to create a mound.

through the candelabra and allowed to trail toward each end of the table. Poppy pods, piñon cones, lavender, and lady apples are worked into the thick rope, and juniper, fresh bayberries, and gold ribbon fill in around the base of the candles themselves. On the Hepplewhite sideboard, ginger jars hold topiaries made of moss-covered craft foam on a moss-wrapped dowel. (The jars are weighted with stones and then filled with craft foam to hold the topiaries in place.) Lady apples and pears are attached with florists' picks. Statice and narcissus sprout from the top, where a three-inch core of the foam has been removed to accommodate a container for the flowers.

In the living room, roping embraces the mirror and mantel, punctuated by arrangements of branches, fruit, and flowers. To create the arrangement over the mirror, Bradley adapted a technique he learned while working with the London floral designers Pulbrook and Gould. He overfilled a papier mâché liner with florists' foam, wrapped chicken wire around both the liner and the florists' foam, then covered this entire foundation with plastic to keep the florists' foam from drying out too quickly. The flower stems are inserted into the foam through the plastic. Florists' wire twisted around the chicken wire forms a hanger for the arrangement, which is suspended from a small eye hook in the crown molding.

The pink strawflowers and rosettes of pineapple foliage give the decorations a floral emphasis that picks up on the rhododendron-covered Bailey & Griffin chintz that dresses sofa and windows. Florals are a signature of Kathleen Riley Sharman's style: Whether decorating her own home or those of her clients, she aims, she says, to create "a lasting springtime." Carrying that theme through even at Christmas yields a refreshing twist on conventional decorations.

The eighteenth-century gilt-framed mirror above the sideboard is an heirloom that has been passed down in Bill Sharman's family. Vases of narcissus on either side of it and in the topiaries on the sideboard below fill the room with heady scent.

Quick-Change Artist

IF YOU WERE TO VISIT THE HOME OF CLARENCE Brooks right before Thanksgiving and then to come back a few weeks later, you might be startled by the transformation. Not only does the Birmingham interior designer put up a tree and hang the stockings with care; he also dresses every love seat, chair, and bench in the living room with special holiday slipcovers. A red cotton with a small white pattern makes a snowflake effect on one love seat. Watered silk moiré is as elegant as a party frock on another. A fauteuil and benches wear box-pleated covers of a plaid Italian velvet. And red silk oriental chair covers slip over the backs of the host and hostess chairs to repeat the Far-Eastern flavor of the Japanese wedding kimono on the wall.

"I love red, particularly for the holidays," says Clarence. And keeping all of the flowers and fabrics in shades of red unifies the various prints and textures. Against the bright yellow walls, the effect is vibrant and bold. Pots of poinsettias supply color at floor level and on tabletops, but Clarence doesn't

Even the furniture is dressed up for the holidays with specially made slipcovers. A cotton fabric, chosen for its snowflake effect, covers the love seat; an Italian velvet plaid covers the benches and fauteuil. A Japanese wedding kimono on the wall adds Christmas color, too.

Instead of flowers, apples "bloom" on bamboo sticks in an arrangement of holly and magnolia. Spray furniture polish gives the fruit and leaves a high sheen. Live poinsettias fill the plaid stocking at the mantel; the root ball is wrapped in a plastic bag, which holds in moisture and keeps the flowers fresh through the season. Above the fireplace, red lanterns frame a nineteenth-century Czechoslovakian painting. The chair in the foreground wears a red silk oriental chair cover, which slips over the chair back.

stop there. "I take them out of the pots, put them in plastic bags, and water them. Then I can use them in arrangements and have them spilling out of the stockings, and they keep through the holidays." Magnolia branches are his other favorite material, and the leaves make a rich foil for pink poinsettias in the dining room.

For Clarence Brooks, his wife, Dottie, and their son, Christopher, the Christmas season always begins with music at McCoy United Methodist Church, where a special choral program to begin Advent is a long-standing tradition. After the Sunday afternoon performance, Clarence's relatives meet at his home for a formal seated dinner. "I'm the first to decorate so the family gathers back here," he says.

The table glitters with silver and gold service plates, crystal trees and reindeer, and vermeil flatware. Lusters, or candelabras hung with glass

"I hide things and pull them out at different times," says Clarence. The gold icon is one of them. "I'm partial to it at Christmas."

Petite pots of azaleas make an enclosure for the Nativity, an unglazed Spanish ceramic puzzle with each figure on a separate piece.

pendants, hold tall white tapers at either end of the table. Clarence says he saw the lusters at a Sotheby's auction and left a sealed bid before returning home. He didn't hear from Sotheby's and forgot about the candelabras until several weeks later, when a box arrived with the lusters carefully packed inside. The unusually tall crystal trees were also a New York find, purchased from a German merchant; the crystal and gold reindeer were an Italian prize, found in a mountain village outside Milan.

Other decorations bring back memories of Christmases past. When Clarence lived in Germany, he followed local tradition and illuminated the tree

with real candles. "I can't do that here," he says, "but I found these candle lights, so they are reminders of three happy Christmases in Germany." The last teddy bear he received as a child has survived in excellent shape, "so I get him out and bedeck him for the holidays, and put him in a prominent place every year." It's a disarmingly sentimental touch in this stylish setting.

The table glitters with a forest of crystal trees, a silver lamé runner, gold and silver service plates, and vermeil flatware. Tureens in the shape of reindeer hold a Brooks family favorite, asparagus soup. On the chest, a white pagoda-shaped tulipière serves as sculpture. In the flanking arrangements, magnolia leaves are a foil for the pink poinsettias, which pick up the color in the vases.

The portrait of Earline Heath King above the Carrara marble mantel was painted by Joseph Wallace King. Love seats face each other over an Italian painted-wood coffee table with a coral-colored marble top.

Accent on Architecture

CHRISTMAS IS SIMPLE AND FAMILY-CENTERED AT Earline Heath King's Winston-Salem, North Carolina, home. "We always have the family dinner here, usually between Christmas and New Year's," she says. "Other than that, there's just the Christmas tree and a collection of ornaments," which have been gathered over the years.

The decorations accent the architecture of the house instead of trying to compete with it. Crystal trees and coral ribbons add a festive touch to the mirrored dining table. A tall Fraser fir and round banquette divide the dining and living areas. A tray filled with yellow statice, baby's-breath, and eucalyptus crowns the banquette, where Earline arranges the "outgoing gifts" that are ready to be delivered.

Above the mantel is Earline's portrait, painted by Joseph Wallace King. Earline is a portraitist herself, but in terra-cotta and bronze rather than canvas and paint. Her commissions include a bronze equestrian statue of R. J. Reynolds that stands near the city hall in Winston-Salem, as well as portrait busts of Dr. Armand Hammer, Winston Churchill, North Carolina Governor James B. Hunt, Jr., and Helen Bonfils, publisher of the Denver *Post* and a patron of the arts.

In light of her commercial success, it is surprising to learn that Earline only discovered her talent for sculpture later in life. "Against my wishes, a friend signed me up for a sculpture workshop twenty-seven years ago," she explains, "and it 'took.' " Winston-Salem is unusually rich in opportunities in the arts, she notes. Once she discovered how much she enjoyed it, she began studying in earnest. She prefers terra-cotta to stone. With stone, "you take away," she explains. "What I do, you start from nothing and add on." Most of her work is commissioned portraiture, but for gallery shows, she does figure sculpture in terra-cotta and bonded bronze or polycast.

Earline's home, built in the early 1950s, incorporates elegant classical details that give the long living-dining room a quiet formality. At each end, a fireplace is framed by a carved Carrara marble mantel, one of a pair that was rescued from an old Baltimore town house.

In contrast to the formal richness of the living room, the study is cozier and more lighthearted. The first thing a visitor notices is the twisted tree trunk near the fireplace. "When we were building, the blight had hit the chestnut trees," Earline explains. Her husband brought one home and stood it in the den; then he painted illusionistic limbs and trunk extending into the "sky" on the ceiling and he added a mural on the fireplace wall behind. "It has been a conversation piece!" says Earline.

Now in her seventies, Earline is represented by galleries and featured in shows across the South and in the West. She recently wrote, "The discovery of creativity in one's self is a joy I wish for everyone. It can't come too early or too late. In one form or another, I truly believe, creativity is within us all—waiting to be liberated."

Fraser fir, magnolia, pinecones, and tiny white lights dress the mantel in the study. The trunk of a chestnut tree killed by the blight appears to extend into an illusionistic sky, thanks to the art of trompe l'oeil.

White woodwork contrasts crisply with the walls, which were recently painted bright yellow over the original "safe beige" flocked paper. A chandelier from Florence, Italy, hangs over the velvet-covered banquette, where gifts await delivery. On the chest beside the tree stands a small Earline Heath King sculpture in terra-cotta.

Too Much Is Just Right

ARTHUR WEEKS LOVED BRIGHT REDS AND LUSCIOUS textures, so Christmas was an obvious time to pull out all the stops. This log cabin was his country retreat and studio in Springville, Alabama, and he decorated it in much the same way that he painted—with vivid color and lots of feeling and flair.

The artist's motto could have been "more is better"—every room in the cabin was filled with things he collected. "He had collections of collections," recalls friend and agent Gene Smith. He bought without regard to provenance or pedigree. "He was able to see the beauty, fun, and elegance in things that other people would have dismissed as junk. He never bought trash—just unloved, unwanted things and made them lovable or wonderful." A crystal chandelier hung from the rafters, and balloon shades dressed the windows in surprising juxtaposition to the glazed-log walls. Layers of rugs were topped with a zebra skin, and a vast collection of miscellaneous plates filled dresser shelves and walls in one corner.

Weeks, now deceased, began painting when he was about eighteen years old and was largely self-taught. His vibrant, boldly brushed canvases of animals, children, gardens, and the cities he visited

Candles, pine, and brass horns dress the rustic fireplace, whose mantel is made of small logs lined up and sawed off evenly. The ungainly pine tree, covered with lights and ornaments, reflects Weeks's flair for turning the unpromising into the unique.

around the world won him an international reputation. In the mid-1960s, some of his paintings were chosen by the State Department for the Art in Embassies program and were exhibited in New Delhi, India.

"Arthur was a great guy who loved life, a bon vivant," says Smith. He experienced people and places in terms of colors, which he would then commit to canvas or paper, evoking his remembered feelings about them. The only example of his work in these photographs is the painted cupboard behind the papier mâché pig (right), but the cabin's interiors express the adventurous spirit with which he approached both life and art.

The cabinet behind the papier mâché pig is decorated with flowers painted by Arthur Weeks.

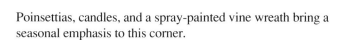

Poinsettias, candles, and a spray-painted vine wreath bring a seasonal emphasis to this corner.

In the Heart of Horse Country

VIRGINIA CAIN CELEBRATED CHRISTMAS AT Virginiana Farm in Kentucky for fifty years, and there were always certain constants: A Christmas Eve supper of escalloped oysters and homemade vegetable soup, followed by midnight Mass at St. Peter's Episcopal Church, then home to bed to wait for Santa Claus.

The centerpiece of decorations was a live Christmas tree that reached to the ceiling, and Virginia remembers her mother spending nearly a week decorating it. In the 1940s, that involved "spraying it pink or blue with calcimine and the vacuum cleaner, spreading angel hair over it to give a halo effect to the lights, hanging silver foil icicles one at a time to look like the tree was dripping with ice. She loved every minute of it," remembers Virginia. Although themes and styles of decorating changed over the years, the tree was always "real and nine feet tall and placed in the living room."

In 1987, that tradition was altered slightly when the Historic Paris-Bourbon County Historical Society asked Virginia to participate in the annual "Christmas Tea in the Country." Because the decorations would have to go up earlier than usual,

Over 1,400 white lights were wired to the branches of the tree to make it "look like a fairyland," says Virginia Cain. The secret to creating the effect, she adds, is to run a strand of lights along each branch from the trunk to the tip and back again.

Virginia bought her first artificial tree. But with the help of interior designer Dwight Cobb, it proved to be spectacular. The tree glittered magically with 1,435 tiny white lights, shiny German glass ornaments, and graceful swags of gold glass beads and peach satin roping caught up with satin bows.

For the rest of the house, they decided on an approach that would be somewhat Victorian but not too formal, "comfortable, warm, and inviting," Virginia explains. To achieve that look, they used dried

German glass peacocks boast real, iridescent tails, with peacock feathers shed by the birds at Virginiana Farm. Miniature musical instruments play off the theme suggested by Virginia Cain's collection of instruments, while handmade tussie-mussies, peach bows, and satin roping produce a lush Victorian look.

The mandolin, violins, and recorder are family pieces. The underpinnings for this lavish arrangement of dried and fresh materials consist of layers of craft foam stacked and taped to the mantel. Designer Dwight Cobb carefully wired the instruments to this foundation, then inserted dried flowers and branches of berry-laden native juniper. Heavy drapery cord and old sheets of music tied with satin ribbons simply rest on the branches.

flowers, fruit, and armloads of greenery from the farm and from friends' gardens. The arrangements were distinctive and eye-catching because of their focal points: musical instruments and sheet music on the living room mantel and a copper hat and hunting horn in the dining room.

"One of the prettiest things, though," says Virginia, "was the bridge." Here, thick garlands of evergreens, held in place with big red velvet bows,

In the centerpiece on the table, a hunting horn, a copper top hat (a reference to the hat in the painting), and fruit rest on a bed of juniper. An English copper coaching horn hangs below the mantel. Above, pewter urns are filled with boxwood and pineapples.

festooned the posts. It was a simple decoration, but one that said "Merry Christmas" to all passersby.

Virginia and her son began a Thoroughbred breeding operation in 1983, but the property had been a working farm for over a century. In 1877, Edwin P. Gamble of Proctor & Gamble Company bought 155 acres from his father for the token sum of one dollar. He built a house on the hill overlooking the Paris-Maysville Turnpike and, with his wife, Elizabeth, raised seven children there before moving to California in 1900. Virginia's parents bought the property in 1937, when she was a student at the University of Kentucky, and christened it with a combination of her first and middle names. In 1990, Virginia sold the farm; but her customs for keeping Christmas go with her, linking her to a life-time of happy holidays at the home place.

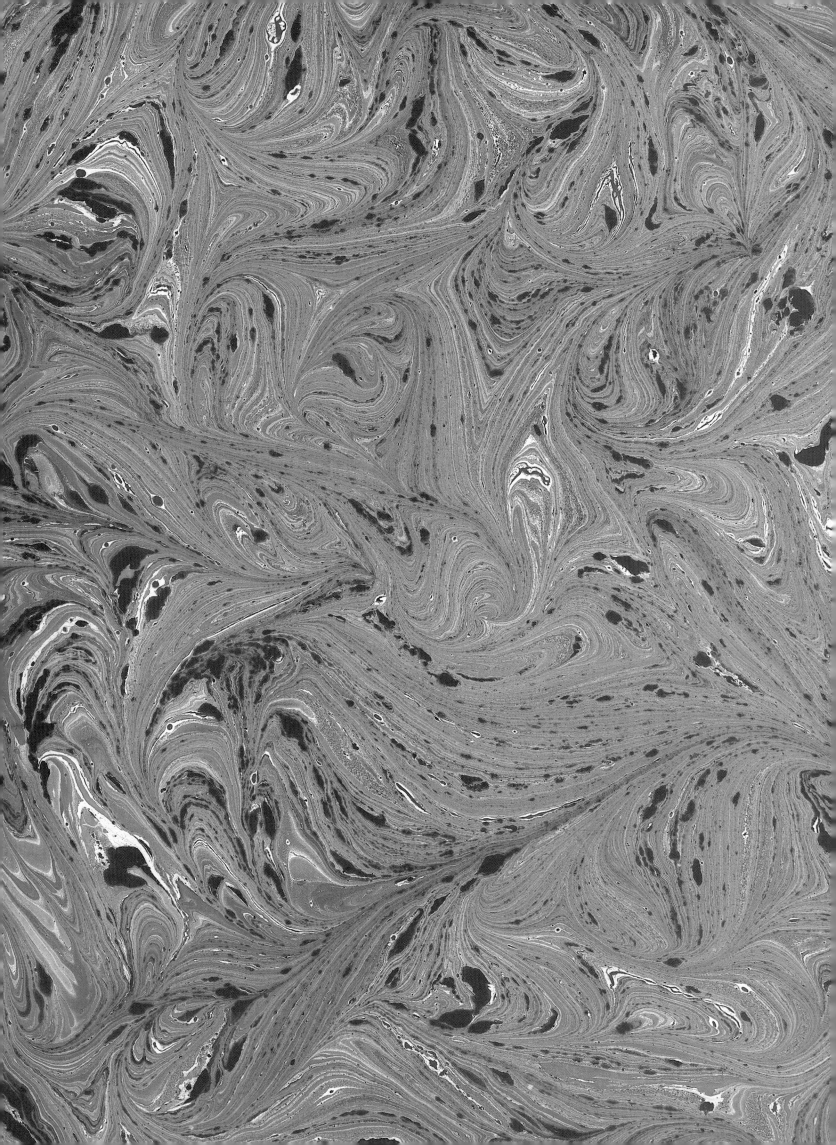

Festive Focus

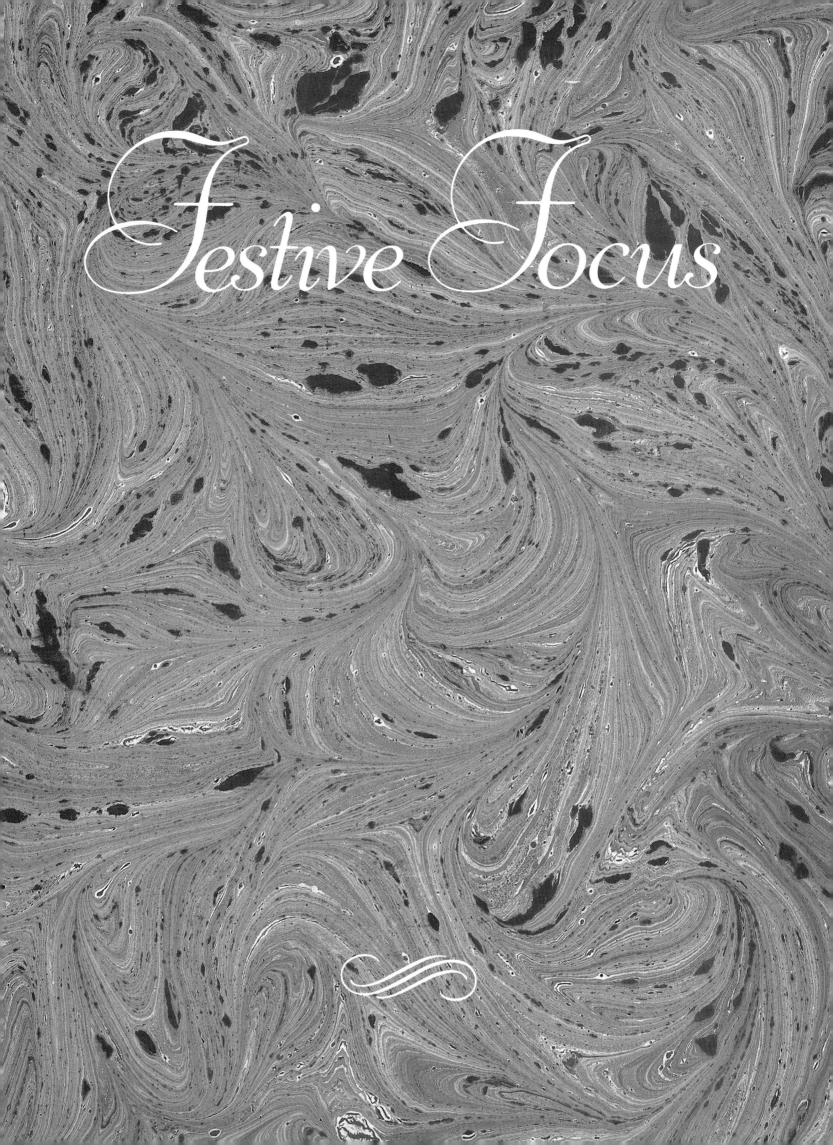

Welcoming the Season

Each house is swept the day before,
And windows stuck with evergreens;
The snow is besomed from the door,
And comfort crowns the cottage scenes.
Gilt holly with its thorny pricks
And yew and box with berries small,
These deck the unused candlesticks,
And pictures hanging by the wall.

—from "Christmas in a Village"
by John Clare (1793-1864)

In Virginia, riding to the hounds has long been part of
Christmas tradition, so what could be a more natural theme
for decorations than the hunt? The festive welcome begins at
the walk, where lampposts wear badges of greenery. The
badges are composed of two bundles of evergreens tied to the
post, with hunting horns wired in place. The red bow hides
the mechanics. Pheasant feathers are simply tucked into the
bunches of greens for an out-of-the-ordinary accent.

A magnolia wreath and overdoor garland offer a sophisticated, quintessentially Southern holiday greeting. The wreath is simple to make. The feathered effect is created by pinning magnolia leaves one at a time to a wreath form (see "Portfolio of Techniques," page 186). Branches of Leyland cypress are inserted at one side to create a gracefully sweeping line, emphasized by the bow and streamers. The asymmetry of the wreath is balanced by that of the overdoor garland, which was assembled in two parts and joined above the center of the door. This ensures that both ends will have a fringe of cypress. Such a thick garland might best be assembled on a plywood base with craft foam wired to it. The magnolia must be inserted as closely as possible to create the bunched fullness seen here. Branches of Leyland cypress are added at the back for softness.

An entrance decorated with wreaths and a spray of greenery has timeless appeal. But add a fountain of white branches in a pedestal planter and suddenly the entrance becomes almost theatrical. Craft foam covered with sphagnum moss provides the foundation for the branches. The spray of greenery on the door (bottom photograph) is made by layering variegated English holly, juniper, and Fraser fir, then wiring them together. Pinecones and fruit are also secured with wire, and a bow, made of plaid ribbon layered over velvet, hides the mechanics. (For an easy method of securing English walnuts to such a spray, see "Portfolio of Techniques," page 189.)

Every year, Dottie Tootle turns her front door into a Christmas package. It is a treatment that is as easy as it is delightful. She simply wraps the length and width of the door with thirty-six-inch-wide velvet and sews the ends together on the inside of the door, being careful to pull the fabric taut. She then pinches the two bands together where they cross in the middle and ties them tightly.

To make the bow, Dottie opens out a length of thirty-six-inch-wide fabric, wrong side up, and spreads tissue paper or newspaper over it to provide stiffness. Then she folds the selvages to the center and stitches the seam closed. Each end is folded into the center, slightly overlapping, pinched tightly in the middle, and tacked securely to form the bow. A fifteen-inch-wide piece of velvet makes the "knot" that attaches the bow to the ribbons on the door. Sometimes Dottie also ties small packages wrapped in white paper and red ribbon to the garland that frames the door and she even carries the theme through to the tree inside.

The trio of wreaths below says "Merry Christmas" Savannah-style. The center one tells the story of cotton, and thus of Savannah's history, with tiny dolls, a ship, and cotton in its various forms from boll to bale. Flanked by twin wreaths made of cotton bolls and husks, it decorates the door of a renovated 175-year-old cotton warehouse, now the home of artist Ann W. Osteen. Assembling a story-telling door decoration with a regional accent may entail something of a treasure hunt to locate the appropriate items. The main things to keep in mind are to choose objects of fairly similar size and scale, and to repeat one or two elements so that the overall effect is unified and harmonious.

An outdoor planter that holds flowers at other times of the year is a perfect spot for an arrangement of fruit and greenery over the holidays. This one can be built up on a cone of craft foam firmly anchored in the planter with florists' tape. Branches of Japanese aucuba are inserted on florists' picks. To keep the foliage fresh longer, wrap the cut ends of the branches in wet cotton puffs before securing them to the pick.

At the top, a pineapple is fastened in place with three six-inch florists' picks. Pears and lemons, inserted with four-inch picks, are grouped by twos, threes, and fours instead of being scattered randomly over the cone. This gives the fruit more impact. To create movement and variety in each grouping, the fruit is positioned at different angles. One pear, for example, points toward the cone, one away from it, and the third is on a diagonal that leads the eye around the arrangement. To finish, hemlock branches are added for a softer, finer texture, and bows of velvet tube ribbon perk up the green and yellow color scheme.

Like an enormous leafy boa, this garland of magnolia and pine frames the front door and curls around the bases of the iron urns, which hold pyramids of apples on moss-covered foundations. Pears and apples are attached in clusters along the length of the garland, and strings of twinkle lights are wrapped among the stems of the greenery.

A few big branches of fir and a huge red bow make a simple starting point for an elegant spray. But to give it more depth and texture against the black door, juniper, white pine, variegated English holly, and clusters of artificial berries are tucked behind and around the bow. Small clusters of berries wired to the ends of the fir branches emphasize the dimensions of the spray.

A long rope of fresh fir outlining the entrance is a traditional starting point for decorating the door. To give the treatment a sophisticated twist, designer Meg Rice added plum-colored paisley bows, strands of gold beads, and bunches of dried millet and wildflowers. Clusters of frosted artificial fruit and shiny red and silver balls bring color and sparkle. The glass balls, fruit, and beads are repeated on the wreath. Instead of completely covering the straw base, Meg used its color and texture as part of the decoration, allowing it to suggest a golden halo for the greenery.

The pediment of the porte cochere continues the hunt theme begun at the walk (see pages 124-25). Here, designer Sheldon Anderson secured the craft foam base to the pediment with wire wound tightly around small nails that were pushed into the joints between the dentil molding and the backboard. Silk holly and fresh evergreens are inserted into the craft foam in a fan shape that radiates from the center of the triangle. The horns, positioned symmetrically to suggest a heraldic device, are attached with florists' wire and picks. Wire-edged ribbon allows the designer to loop and shape the streamers for a lively effect.

The badges, or plaques, for which Colonial Williamsburg is famous are usually made with evergreens and fruit, but creative designers seem never to run out of new combinations and presentations. These three badges, designed by Claude Jones, are built on a foundation of florists' foam. To make the corner arrangements, branches of Noble fir are inserted to define half circles. Stems of artemisia and pinecones wired to florists' picks are added next, then yarrow and an ornamental pineapple. The yarrow is positioned so that a guest at the door looks up into the flower faces. The pineapples are placed so that the rosettes of foliage face each other, but at different angles to avoid stiffness.

The center badge is constructed in much the same way, with fir and artemisia establishing the main lines. To give greater depth to the design, the pineapple foliage points outward and the yarrow faces up, out, and down, following the primary lines. Birch twigs inserted at the bottom edge add a delicate line to loosen the dense, compact effect of the greenery.

Shed antlers found in the woods and a tangle of wild vines give a distinctly Southwestern look to this entry. But the fruiting vines are unlike anything you will see in nature. Silk Japanese maple leaves, canella berries, dried gourds dyed red, and sugar pinecones have been attached to a grapevine frame to punctuate its gestural line with shape, texture, and color. Sumac berries and juniper branches hint at traditional holiday materials, and copper paper-twist ribbon wraps the whole with gleaming style. To avoid damaging the stucco wall with nails, the piece was assembled as a unit in the workshop and suspended over the door from wires attached to eye hooks in the wooden beam overhead.

Pillar and door decorations in the Williamsburg style combine magnolia leaves, boxwood, and fruit for a look that is formal and restrained. The designer made the badges long enough to cover a little more than half the length of the pillars so that they could be seen easily from the street. The simplest way to construct them is on a craft foam base. Magnolia leaves can be applied with fern pins, and both fruit and boxwood can be inserted on florists' picks (see "Portfolio of Techniques," pages 187-88).

The scale of this door, with its oversized swan-neck pediment, requires decorations that are similarly proportioned. Accordingly, the wreath fills the top half of the door, and the badges stretch from the base of the pediment down to the shrubbery that frames the entrance. Branches of fir are the basis for both decorations, with bunches of juniper added for contrasting texture. Fresh pears, apples, and limes are secured with florists' picks, along with bleached and natural pinecones. Nut clusters (see "Portfolio of Techniques," page 189) and artificial grapes complete the wreath. To make the big red velvet bows, the designer tied loose knots along the length of the ribbon so that when the bow was made, the knots shaped it in unexpected ways. Knots in the streamers make a finishing flourish.

Just two kinds of foliage, juniper and magnolia leaves, are used to decorate this door. To make the evergreen frame, staple magnolia leaves to 1 x 2 strips of wood that can be attached to the door frame with small nails. The juniper rope can then be stapled or wired on top of the magnolia leaves.

The wreaths are easy to assemble on craft foam wreath forms. (Straw forms may be pulled out of shape by the weight of the fruit.) Fern pins secure the magnolia leaves to the back of the form. Then bunches of juniper, wired to florists' picks, are inserted along the front and inner and outer edges of the form (see "Portfolio of Techniques," pages 184-85). Juniper covers slightly more than half of the circle, and chinaberries cover the rest. Florists' picks also hold the apples in place, evenly spaced around the wreath.

To give this entrance impact even from a distance, floral designer Bob Strother made an oversized wreath for the door and swagged the stair rail with a fruit-studded garland. The wreath looks especially generous because it is built up on a six-inch-wide straw base with a flat cardboard backing. (The backing helps keep the wreath form from sagging out of shape.) After sprigging in the boxwood, Strother inserts apples and pinecones on florists' picks. He recommends Staymen or Winesap apples for outdoor arrangements; they stay fresh-looking longer than Red Delicious in the warm, damp weather that is typical in December over much of the South.

The garland is assembled with spool wire and incorporates a variety of materials, including Fraser fir, pine, juniper, and magnolia (see "Portfolio of Techniques," page 183). The resulting rope is so thick that apples and pinecones can be secured to it using only florists' picks.

Oyster shells give this badge a Tidewater flavor. Holly and juniper are inserted in a foundation of florists' foam to create the green background for the pomegranates and shells. Florists' wire pushed through the pomegranates and bent into a U shape will hold the fruit in place. The shells can be attached to florists' picks with a little florists' clay.

Deck the Halls

So now is come our joyful'st feast;
Let every man be jolly.
Each room with ivy-leaves is dressed,
And every post with holly.
Though some churls at our mirth repine
Round your foreheads garlands twine,
Drown sorrow in a cup of wine,
And let us all be merry.

—from "Our Joyful'st Feast"
by George Wither (1588-1667)

Wreaths and swags, a kissing ball, and a bustle of greenery on
the newel all work together to transform this entrance hall for
Christmas. At the head of the stairs, a vine wreath sprayed
gold is layered over a fir wreath for a bright accent. At the
newel, a bird's nest is perched atop the greenery, and
poinsettias surround the Regency-style dummy board.

Bowls filled with bare branches and silk poinsettias step down to the floor, where pots of live flowers bring the line forward in a graceful curve. The grouping of real and artificial plants in this way fills the corner with color and helps to lead the eye upward to the Nativity on top of the chest.

To make an ordinary pine swag more interesting, layer it with ropes of fresh cranberries and multicolored metallic braid. Here the ropes are draped in irregular loops over the white pine garland for a loose, graceful line that is both casual and elegant. The bouquet of florists' flowers on the newel is arranged in a basket filled with florists' foam and wrapped in heavy foil.

Branches of white pine, wired together to form roping, have a languid quality that is underscored by the deep loops of the garland. Strands of pearl and gold beads twisted together overlay the loops to highlight them, and the red velvet bows that catch up the garland have long streamers to emphasize the elegant sweep of the greenery.

On the stair, opposite, a papier mâché angel hovers. The homeowner sprayed the cherub gold and added the nosegay and barrettes of dried rosebuds and statice. Lotus and other dried pods sprayed gold are fastened to the newel itself to punctuate the beginning of the handrail.

Alexandrian laurel (*Danae racemosa*), known as ruscus in the florists' trade, lends itself to decorating an interior arch because the stems are long and flexible and can be twined around each other to make a long "branch" with a gracefully sweeping line. A plastic cage filled with florists' foam and hung on a small nail in the molding provides the foundation for the central arrangement of pyracantha berries, variegated English holly, and English laurel. Additional Alexandrian laurel and English holly are secured at the corners of the arch for a flowing line. The garland covers only one-third of the door frame; greenery and nandina berries add a flourish to the flanking sconces and carry the eye down to the chair rail.

A collar of evergreens and pinecones emphasizes the arched doorway in the President's House at the College of William and Mary. The collar is made by stapling Noble fir and holly to a plywood base, then hot-gluing white pine and spruce cones along the center. The base is actually four shaped pieces, two on each side, attached to the woodwork with finishing nails at the top and bottom of each piece.

A cupboard that normally displays china can be partly cleared for the holidays to make room for a Christmas collection like these reindeer. The pair of Indian lacquered and gilded deer are actually boxes, the marionette is antique, and the slender bronze pair in the center was found in a San Francisco department store. The exotic character of these reindeer harmonizes so well with the style of the figures painted on the Portuguese platter that the homeowner decided to display it here as well. The four densely patterned plates on the shelf below are part of a dinner service from Japan. A rope of white pine swags the top of the cupboard, which is crowned with a straw reindeer, pepper berries, and eucalyptus.

The wreath above and left celebrates its Florida origins with calamondin oranges and palmetto cones. Designer Lucille Maloney started with a standard wreath form to which she pinned magnolia leaves, overlapping them around the form. (Polishing the leaves first with a wool cloth will give them a sheen.) Bits of Spanish moss soften the outside edges. Clusters of juniper, Burford holly berries, calamondin oranges, and palmetto cones are then secured with wire or wooden picks. The palmetto cones are made by slitting a green palmetto leaf into four sections and double-plaiting them; the cone shape forms automatically. Originally used in Central Florida as Palm Sunday decorations, the cones are now popular at Easter and Christmas, too.

For a creative twist on the traditional fruit-and-greenery wreath, designer Tucker Renfrow halved two apples and added them around the inside edge of the wreath. The flat cross section of the fruit makes a pleasing contrast to the round shapes of oranges, lemons, limes, and whole apples. To keep the cut surfaces from browning, Renfrow dipped them in lemon juice and wrapped the halves tightly in plastic wrap before securing them with florists' picks. The same idea could work with lemons and oranges, too, although these are a little juicier than apples and would need to be well blotted on paper towels before being wrapped in plastic.

There's no rule that says all ornaments must hang from cone-shaped evergreen trees. The lichen-covered branches at right offer interesting texture and line, with lots of twigs for hanging toy soldiers and for draping the star garland in sweeping loops. Fine gold bullion wire strung among the stars catches the light and gives the effect of spider webs or angel hair.

Variegated-ivy topiary standards, built on craft foam balls covered with sphagnum moss, sport airy crowns of lilies, roses, and alstroemeria. Boughs of Noble fir, eucalyptus, and fresh fruit form a colorful tapestry on the table below.

Popcorn wreaths are a specialty of the Gullah people, descendants of West Africans who settled in the coastal areas of South Carolina, Georgia, and North Florida. The "popcorn" is the mature seed of the Chinese tallow tree, which grows in coastal South Carolina and across the Gulf South and Lower South to Texas. The Gullahs tie bunches of the seeds together to make long strands, which they weave into wreaths. For this tabletop display, small wreaths are placed on top of two larger ones, and candles are set in the centers.

Fiery colors and imported, long-stemmed fresh peppers give this holiday arrangement a south-of-the-border feeling. You can use either potted or cut amaryllis in such an arrangement, although using potted ones will require a basket large enough for both the pots and the container that holds the other flowers. For cut amaryllises, some florists recommend filling the hollow stem with water and plugging it with cotton before placing it in the arrangement. Because the stems are so large, it might be easier to arrange them in a container filled with crumpled chicken wire than in florists' foam.

An ivy basket filled with tulips and lilies is the kind of decoration that doubles as an excellent gift. The florists' flowers can be replaced when they fade, or the ivy basket can be used by itself as a living topiary. A wire basket holds the pot of ivy, which is trained around the sides and over the handle. (It may take a year for the ivy to cover the basket.) The flowers are inserted in water picks, which are pushed into the soil.

A wire topiary form is the starting point for this whimsical centerpiece of airborne Santas. Anchored in a basket weighted for stability and filled with florists' foam and sphagnum moss, the form is embellished with ribbons, bows, cording, and greenery and hung with Santas in hot-air balloons. The Santa in the center of the basket is a music box that plays "Here Comes Santa Claus."

Set the Stage for Dining

The table was literally loaded with good cheer, and presented an epitome of country abundance, in this season of overflowing larders.

—from *The Sketch Book* by Washington Irving

The wandering lines of corkscrew willow, a tangle of bittersweet, and a fallen bird's nest give a wild and spontaneous quality to this dining table centerpiece. To compose an arrangement like this, it is important to start with a foundation of florists' foam that projects well above the rim of the container so that pine, magnolia leaves, and nandina berries can be angled toward the tabletop. This links the arrangement visually to the surface of the table. Gnarled pine branches, collected from the woods, and corkscrew willow balance this downward thrust with lines that lift up and out. Florists' flowers—star-of-Bethlehem, white freesia, paperwhite narcissus, red and white tulips, and red roses—provide the transition between the two and supply the Christmassy color scheme.

This table runner of greenery is a variation of dining table decorations seen in a number of historic houses in Maryland and Virginia. Several long pieces of ivy are tied together at the cut end and braided to form a leafy rope, which is then sprigged with English boxwood and nandina berries for fullness. Placing the runner on a wide ribbon protects the table and sets off the greenery. A dried palmetto fan trimmed to fit the proportions of the table is placed at each end of the runner as a finishing flourish.

The focal point of the dining table is a simple centerpiece in an antique epergne. Pomegranates are stacked in the top bowl with bits of English boxwood and nandina berries tucked around them. In the two lower bowls, florists' foam provides the foundation for rounded arrangements of boxwood, nandina berries, and "dove tails," cream-colored silk moiré folded in half and wired to a florists' pick.

A trio of sugarplum trees brings the feeling of a fantasy forest to this dining table. Each tree starts with a craft foam cone. To protect the Imari bowls from damage and to make the trees portable, designer Daniel Hawks pushed a dowel into the center of each cone, leaving enough of the dowel extending to secure it in a candleholder, which rests in the bowl. A tall candle could be used instead of a dowel to achieve the same result.

Sprigs of varying lengths of American boxwood are pinned onto the cone with fern pins and positioned to give the tree naturalistic dimension and depth. Hawks then sprayed the tree with lacquer and sprinkled the leaves liberally with sugar to create the snow-covered effect. To complete the tree, kumquats, dried apricots, dried pear halves, and prunes are secured on heavy florists' wire and inserted into the cone. Short stems of bittersweet and Blue Mystery weed (a dyed dried grass available from craft shops) are also added to emphasize the colors in the Imari bowls. Garlands of golden raisins strung on heavy cotton thread provide the finishing touch.

A simple topiary in a silver bowl makes an elegant centerpiece for a small table. The trunk is tall enough to lift the greenery above the guests' line of vision, which also keeps the table from feeling cluttered. The topiary is not difficult to make. A ball of craft foam or florists' foam pushed onto a fairly straight tree branch provides the foundation for the topiary, which is made here with artificial boxwood and holly berries. The trunk may be anchored in florists' clay or in florists' foam weighted with rocks and covered with sphagnum moss.

The table decoration at left and below proves that you do not need armloads of expensive flowers to create a spectacular effect. The drama here starts with long tree branches that sweep up toward the ceiling from arrangements on either side of the table's center. The arrangements are loosely constructed, airy combinations of hemlock branches, a few miniature carnations and anthuriums, and bare sticks to which gilded leaves and metallic clusters of grapes have been glued. To link the two, a fat rope of artificial pine falls from the rim of each vase to meet at the center arrangement. This is surprisingly simple, with hemlock and fir defining the shape. Color comes from the anthuriums, miniature carnations, and an ornamental pineapple. Glittery packages and artificial fruits and leaves provide sparkle.

According to designer J. Potter Paul, garnishing paintings and mirrors with greenery is an old Southern custom. It is one he still finds useful, especially in rooms with high ceilings. The architecture leads the eye upward, and to give it something to focus on, he decorates the chandelier as well as the painting over the mantel. Here, Fraser fir branches are simply tucked behind the nineteenth-century Italian mirror, forming a mesh that helps secure the statice, bamboo twigs, and lemons on florists' picks. Matching arrangements on each side of the mirror bring the eye down to the mantel.

No real hostess would ever ask her guests to peer through such a thicket of amaryllises and tulips, but this floral fantasy at the Alliance Children's Theatre Guild Christmas House in Atlanta does contain some ideas for special-occasion decorating. For a party that demands theatrical extravagance, for example, the entire centerpiece would translate well to a side table or buffet. The flowers and a head of ornamental cabbage are arranged in glass bowls placed inside vine baskets. Pots of variegated ivy are banked against the arrangement to provide transition from the basket edge to the table.

Spring flowers at Christmas are a luxury. But tulips are so expressive that you do not need many for an effective arrangement. Here, less than two dozen magenta tulips have simply been placed in faux-malachite glass vases and allowed to turn and fall as they please. Between them, a ceramic bowl holds clusters of magnolia leaves and silver and magenta glass balls.

The colors may be traditional, but the strongly architectural quality of the flowers creates a sophisticated, untraditional effect. The arrangement is actually a cluster of plants: bromeliads in mirrored vases hide a third container in which the pink ginger, calla lilies, anthuriums, and orchids are arranged.

More than one partridge roosts in this tree of dried German statice. The pedestal, with tiny wooden pear trees under each arch, is a Brett Landenberger design, made of handpainted paper applied to wood. The tree itself is made with a craft foam cone. Fern pins secure the double strands of pearls, gold ribbons, and bows, and birds are carefully wedged among the statice. Embossed paper birds on wires are reproductions of antique pieces.

To raise flowers above the eye level of guests at a New Year's dinner, designer Cliff Lassahn built his own pedestal, using wooden dowels nailed to square pieces of wood and painted gold. Pine and holly hide the base, and a shallow container filled with florists' foam rests on the top to hold the arrangement of pine, holly, fir, and lilies. The beauty of this pedestal, besides its easy construction, is that it could be finished in a number of ways—painted solid black, marbleized, or given a faux-granite finish, for example.

Real poinsettias require special treatment for cutting and arranging, and they do not last long. Fortunately, silk ones that make convincing and convenient substitutes are readily available. Combining them with artificial fir and berried branches in a honeysuckle-vine basket shaped like a sleigh produces a casual centerpiece for this holiday table. The berries emphasize the horizontals and diagonals of the arrangement. Including several types of branches provides variety of scale, which makes the design more pleasing.

The most basic rule for decorating the dining table is based on simple thoughtfulness: The centerpiece should be either low enough or high enough to be out of the line of sight between guests on opposite sides of the table. This centerpiece does both. Silver candelabras, fitted with epergnettes, lift arrangements of pineapples, boxwood, and apples well above the tabletop (see "Portfolio of Techniques," pages 190-91). Balancing the fruit properly on the candelabra is critical; otherwise, the arrangement will fall over.

Because the pineapples carry the eye to the chandelier above, designer Bob Strother drew it into the composition with bits of greenery tucked among the arms. To keep the arrangements from looking top-heavy, he built a wreath around the base of each candelabra, using florists' foam, short sprigs of boxwood, and lady apples on florists' picks.

The center arrangement is a conventional design whose tallest amaryllis is level with the base of the pineapple's boxwood collar, but the remaining materials—gerbera daisies, holly, fir, corkscrew willow, protea, winterberry, and yellow roses—quickly step down toward the table so that the arrangement does not obstruct conversation.

Memorable Mantels

Up flew the bright sparks in myriads as the logs were stirred, and the deep red blaze sent forth a rich glow, that penetrated into the furthest corner of the room, and cast its cheerful tint on every face.

—from *Posthumous Papers of the Pickwick Club* by Charles Dickens

With apples and fresh greenery on the mantel, a room will smell as Christmassy as it looks. Using a mixture of greenery provides a variety of textures, which makes the wreath and garland more interesting visually. The combination of fruit and greenery can be dressed up or down. Strings of popcorn give the wreath and mantel a country-casual look; gold beads or pearls would make it more formal.

Red moiré ribbon gives this mantel decoration its punch. Big bows with streamers serve as the focal point for each greenery arrangement and catch up the swag above the fireplace. Instead of wrapping the garland, ribbons ripple along its length, strengthening the impact of color against the greenery and the dark wood of the mantel.

The idea of a Christmas hunt inspired this composition. All of the items are balanced on the pair of books and carved fox head at the center. Clusters of artificial berries are positioned to suggest spiraled roping, and old drapery cording and tassels wind over the pheasant and around the lamp for a luxurious effect.

The simplest recipe for a Christmas mantel can also be the best. The essential ingredients are a fresh wreath, candlelight, and lots of red and green. Grouping unmatched candlesticks of various heights at each end of the mantel creates an informal symmetry. Big red bows on the wreath and at each end of the mantel add softness, and holly serves as a frame. Dried hydrangea, pinecones, and berries are simply scattered along the mantel to fill out the decoration.

Potted plants are the starting point for the decoration, opposite, a treatment that delivers a lot of elegance for a minimal investment of time and money. Pots of amaryllis flank a large Christmas cactus with peach-colored flowers, and smaller cacti beneath the Waterford sconces frame the amaryllises. The center pot also serves as a foundation for gold-sprayed corkscrew willow and nandina foliage, which are carefully wedged into the soil around the plant. Potted miniature ivy supplies long, trailing vines that hide all the containers and cascade like streamers over the mantel.

Trompe l'oeil topiaries are such an eye-catching focal point that the decoration above is kept simple so as not to detract from them. A rope of pine and hemlock lies on the mantel, with juniper branches piled on top to create a thick blanket around the ginger jars. Pots of orchids frame the chimney breast, while lemons and little vases of yellow and white flowers pick up the hues of the walls and trim. A pot of pink-and-white poinsettias is slipped into a basket to fill the empty fireplace with colors that echo those in the topiaries. Whelk shells serve as a clever accessory for the flowers, flanking them like andirons and linking them to the topiaries.

A ribbon-wrapped garland makes a festive frame for the painting over the mantel, and adding gilded sycamore and sweet gum leaves gives the treatment distinction. Gilding leaves is easy: simply spray fallen leaves with enamel spray paint. You might want to experiment with different brands of paint, because some golds are more bronze, while others are brighter and more yellow in tone.

Suspended against an expanse of mirror, this arrangement seems to float in mid-air. The secret is in the mechanics, a plastic cage filled with florists' foam and equipped with a suction cup that adheres to smooth surfaces. One drawback to using the device is that watering is virtually impossible without making a mess; so it is best to use it for decorations that will be in place only a short time or for those made of long-lasting materials. Most of the ones in this spray—juniper, fir, winterberry, protea, corkscrew willow, and galax—will hold up well even after the florists' foam dries out.

Monofilament and suction cups make magic possible on this mirrored chimney breast. Artificial and fresh garlands are wrapped with pink plaid ribbon and hung from the ceiling molding with monofilament. (The artificial pine is included to add gold highlights.) Italian wooden angels are attached to the mirror with suction cups, and florists' foam is wedged above them to hold greenery from the garden and artificial fruit. Anthuriums and carnations supply color. To make the flowers last longer, designer Mary Elam inserted each into a water pick, which she then secured in the florists' foam. The arrangements, framing an antique mirror, hang asymmetrically to make the composition more dynamic, and streamers looped toward them from the central bow provide a graceful, luxuriant effect.

Wire-edged ribbon and strands of stars on foil-wrapped wire allow you to create special effects with very little effort. Simply wrapping the stars around the garland produces sparkling constellations at the fireplace. To fix the ribbon into waves and curls, try shaping it around something cylindrical—a pencil for very tight curls, for example, or a rolling pin for looser ones.

With its rich combination of nuts, seeds, cones, pods, and dried materials, this mantel swag in the Nathaniel Russell House in Charleston evokes the woods, fields, and farms of the South. Although the Spanish moss roping may have to be replaced after a couple of seasons, the pendant can be stored for use year after year. Adding fresh holly and juniper each Christmas enlivens it with color.

Designer Dan Flannery used silk Scotch pine garlands on the mantel and along the back of the sofa as a foundation for natural materials—baby's-breath, Spanish moss, statice, bittersweet, and pinecones. Shiny blue balls supply highlights.

It took designer Eleanor Weller fourteen hours to weave this magnificent garland, using a twenty-foot-long piece of rope and more than four dozen varieties of greenery, nuts, berries, seedpods, and dried flowers. Working from both ends toward the middle ensured that flower faces and branches would fall in the same direction on both sides of the mantel. For the basic technique of assembling a garland, see "Portfolio of Techniques," page 183.

Glittering trees made of foil-wrapped branches and hung with gold ornaments add a festive touch to a collection of blanc-de-chine figures. On the mantel, figures and votive candles are lined up below the gilded Spanish altarpiece, which is embellished with greenery for the season.

A porcelain bisque Nativity occupies the place of honor on the mantel, framed by narcissus and antique Chinese vases filled with fir. The mirrors above are real, reflecting a fifteen-foot tree covered with four thousand lights, but the chinoiserie frame is not—it is a piece of deception created with paint. Real gilded sconces enhance the illusion.

Even without a mantel, the fireplace is the natural focal point for decorating. The ceiling beam is a bonus, another chance to reinforce the colors, textures, and lines of the mantel swag. Here, boxwood roping is the foundation for the garlands, which are sprigged with eucalyptus, dried hydrangea, artemisia, and pepper berries. Gilded and black angels accent the swag on the ceiling beam, while hunting horns and white porcelain cherubs form the focal point above the fireplace.

This pinecone garland, made by floral designer Becky Baxter, was inspired by one at Carter's Grove, near Williamsburg. Becky's husband cut the swagged shape from pegboard; then Becky attached pinecones with a hot-glue gun. Dried celosia, pomegranates, pods, and nut clusters were also hot-glued in place. Each year after hanging the garland, the Baxters tuck in sprigs of boxwood around the pinecones to give the swag a softer edge.

Magnolia branches often seem to arrange themselves. These were chosen for their interesting lines and were wired to nails driven into the mortar between the chimney stones. A big bow and yards of velvet ribbon that wind casually through the branches give the design a holiday look. After Christmas, the homeowner left the branches in place and allowed the leaves to dry to a warm brown, for a sculptural effect to enjoy year-round.

Evoking *The Nutcracker* ballet, a collection of nutcrackers and mice take over the mantel. Bare branches that have been sprayed white fill the urns to provide a wintry look without hiding the painting or overwhelming the little army below.

Some of the ornaments that would ordinarily hang on the tree, such as dolls, toys, and musical instruments, can be assembled on the mantel instead. Add dollhouse furniture and tiny packages, and you have Santa's toy shop in miniature, a lighthearted alternative to traditional fruit and greenery.

For a home in which pride in Texas heritage is on display all year, seasonal decorations simply embellish what is already there. A red-and-gold metallic garland weaves a path among the candles on the mantel, in front of a row of Indian pottery. One tall candle tied with red cotton drapery cord serves as a focal point.

The Well-Trimmed Tree

At a signal from my mother, we followed her into the dining room on the other side of the passage. . . on the table in the centre there was placed a great Christmas Tree hung all over with little lamps and bon-bons and toys and sweetmeats and bags of cakes. It was the first tree of the kind that I and my companions had ever seen.

—from *Christmas Tree*, 1857

Bittersweet, baby's-breath, and statice tucked among the branches give this tree a soft, airy look. Instead of a star, a bunch of bittersweet tops the tree, and velvet ribbon is twisted and curled among the branches to serve as a garland. Although dried materials often suggest an informal country style, their combination here with shiny blue balls creates a suitably sophisticated look.

European splendor was designer Becky Dossey's goal when she decorated this tree for the Kappa Kappa Gamma Houston Christmas Pilgrimage. To top the tree, she created a bubble-like cluster of glass balls by hot-gluing the ornaments to a craft foam sphere that she first painted dark green. A dowel in the bottom of the sphere is aligned with the trunk and wired to it (the top of the tree had to be removed to make room for the cluster). Yards of gold lamé are wrapped loosely around the trunk, both to hide the dowel and to give depth and dimension to the tree.

Instead of swagging the ropes of beads around the tree in the usual way, Becky Dossey draped them over the branches so that they would fall in loops, like necklaces. The effect is equally graceful and easier to manage than swags.

Volunteers made the Victorian-style ornaments that decorate the tree, opposite, in the front hall of the Richards-DAR House Museum in Mobile, Alabama. Lace fans, red cornucopias filled with mints, and baskets and gold-sprayed doilies with ribbon roses and baby's-breath are simple to make but give an impression of old-fashioned elegance. Paper doilies also back the red bows that secure the pine garland to the banister, underscoring the tree's lacy theme.

Most of the ornaments on this ten-foot-tall tree are German, some dating to 1870, when a German glassmaker invented molded glass ornaments. The owner started with ornaments from his mother's childhood tree and those she collected when he was growing up, and then in the 1970s and 1980s, he began actively searching for antique and unusual ornaments himself. The earliest are egg-shaped *kugels,* the first true Christmas ornaments, made in the 1840s. German craftsmen soon developed thousands of forms, including flowers, fruits, vegetables, animals and birds, elves, umbrellas, coffee pots, and teapots.

Near the glass peach, far right, is a fantasy ornament, a house with four bells hanging from it. Above the ear of corn is an early glass cauldron, which held oil and a floating wick to illuminate the tree.

The more crocheted snowflakes you have on the tree, the better. Here, the homeowner used a variety of patterns, but all are about the same size. Combining different sizes is also effective, provided you use a full range, from large to medium to small. For crocheters, these snowflakes are wonderful projects to give as gifts or to keep, building a collection that will eventually cover the tree.

An Oriental fishbowl offers a novel solution to the problem of displaying a live tree. The bowl has been weighted with sand and outfitted with a form to hold the root ball and keep the tree upright. Because the fishbowl is watertight, the root ball can be kept moist until it is time to plant the tree outside. To help a live tree survive until planting, keep it in a cool room, out of drafts. Use small twinkle lights instead of large bulbs, which produce more heat and dry out the needles more. And try not to keep the tree indoors longer than ten days. Otherwise, the warm air can cause it to break dormancy; then when you plant it outside, the cold air might kill it.

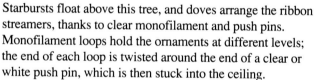

Starbursts float above this tree, and doves arrange the ribbon streamers, thanks to clear monofilament and push pins. Monofilament loops hold the ornaments at different levels; the end of each loop is twisted around the end of a clear or white push pin, which is then stuck into the ceiling.

A game table normally stands under the chandelier in this den, but for Christmas it is moved out of the way so that the tree can wear a crown of lights and ribbons. Bunches of artificial greenery and berries are secured to red velvet bows with long streamers and wired to the chandelier. Additional lengths of ribbon are then hung over the chandelier arms and allowed to curl and fall down the tree.

A stair landing can be a good place for a nostalgic Christmas vignette. Here, a small fresh fir forms the centerpiece, and a collection of antique toys, doll's dresser and bed, small blanket chests, and a child's cart are arranged around it as if Santa had just left. Even if you do not have such a generous stair landing, the same decorating idea can work in any empty corner that needs a festive touch. Use a small tree and assemble old toys, stuffed teddy bears, old books, and baskets at the base of the tree. The guidelines for painting a still life apply: Choose a variety of shapes and sizes for interest, but be sure to repeat shapes and sizes for unity. Arranging them in a fairly orderly progression of sizes from front to back will lead the eye to the tree, but putting something small and low closer to the tree will add interest and make the display more effective.

Camel cookies have double symbolism on this tree at Graylyn, built in 1927 by the president of R. J. Reynolds Tobacco Company. Besides being the Wise Men's mode of transportation to Bethlehem, they represent the tobacco company's famous logo. Bouquets of dried flowers—hydrangea, yarrow, goldenrod, money plant, strawflowers, cock's-comb, statice, and dusty miller—are tied with red ribbons and secured to the branches for colorful everlasting ornaments. The tree stands in the Persian card room, carefully restored in 1983 to reveal walls paneled in nineteenth-century handcarved, gessoed, and gilded wood that came from Istanbul.

For this family, decorating the tree is literally a time for remembering special people and special times. The only ornaments are dozens of family photos in small gold-colored picture frames. Most of the frames are the kind made for framing cross-stitch ornaments, so they are inexpensive, lightweight, and easy to hang.

A glitzy pink and gold tree with matching packages is an unconventional alternative to the usual red and green. Ostrich feathers dyed two shades of pink are inserted among the branches, placed so that they seem to sprout from the tree itself. The collection of balls and bells plays up the gold and pink theme, which carries through to the packages. These are decorated with gold mesh, lamé, and ribbons shredded with a ribbon shredder.

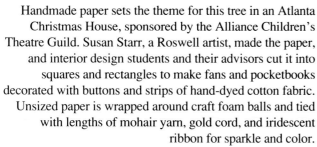

Handmade paper sets the theme for this tree in an Atlanta Christmas House, sponsored by the Alliance Children's Theatre Guild. Susan Starr, a Roswell artist, made the paper, and interior design students and their advisors cut it into squares and rectangles to make fans and pocketbooks decorated with buttons and strips of hand-dyed cotton fabric. Unsized paper is wrapped around craft foam balls and tied with lengths of mohair yarn, gold cord, and iridescent ribbon for sparkle and color.

While an enormous Christmas tree in the living room is often the centerpiece of a home's decorations and a family's celebrations, the idea of using several small trees throughout the house is increasingly popular. Here, in a corner of the front parlor, one such tree and piles of packages become part of the festive backdrop for holiday entertaining. The tree is raised on a mirrored pedestal, and the ornaments are limited to just a few kinds: white lights, mirrored prisms, papier mâché angels, and gold ribbon. In addition, bare branches of deciduous huckleberry have been sprayed silver and wedged carefully among the fir boughs to loosen the compact shape of the tree with sketchy, gestural lines. To keep the tree from looking like an isolated column, designer Tucker Renfrow created visual transition to the floor with a pyramid of foil-wrapped packages and a collection of white poinsettias.

In another variation on the idea of limiting colors and kinds of ornaments, this tree becomes an icy spectacle, with twenty-two strands of white lights, one thousand crystal icicles, and a collection of clear glass ornaments.

Hundreds of lights, glittering metallic ribbon, and shiny glass balls produce a jewel-encrusted effect on this tree. There are only a few types of ornaments, however. The richness comes from the colors and textures: balls in shades of plum, mauve, and magenta as well as white and gold; beaded hearts; and bows of metallic, lace, and moiré ribbon. The bows are made by layering contrasting ribbon—red moiré and white lace or silver and gold—and tying them into a bow. The plum and mauve palette of the tree carries through the room, even to the packages spread on the floor, which are wrapped in colored foils and ribbons like those on the tree.

Since tulle is one of Phyllis George Brown's favorite decorating materials for special occasions, her decorator, Mark Eliason, uses yards of it to festoon the tree that dominates the great room, opposite. Red and gold ribbons are swagged with it to add color and sparkle to the veils of white. Red bows are also tied to branch tips, a simple way to give a festive look to the tree and to unify a varied collection of ornaments. The Browns' ornaments include the unusual motif of chickens—he co-founded Kentucky Fried Chicken and she is chairman and founder of Chicken By George.

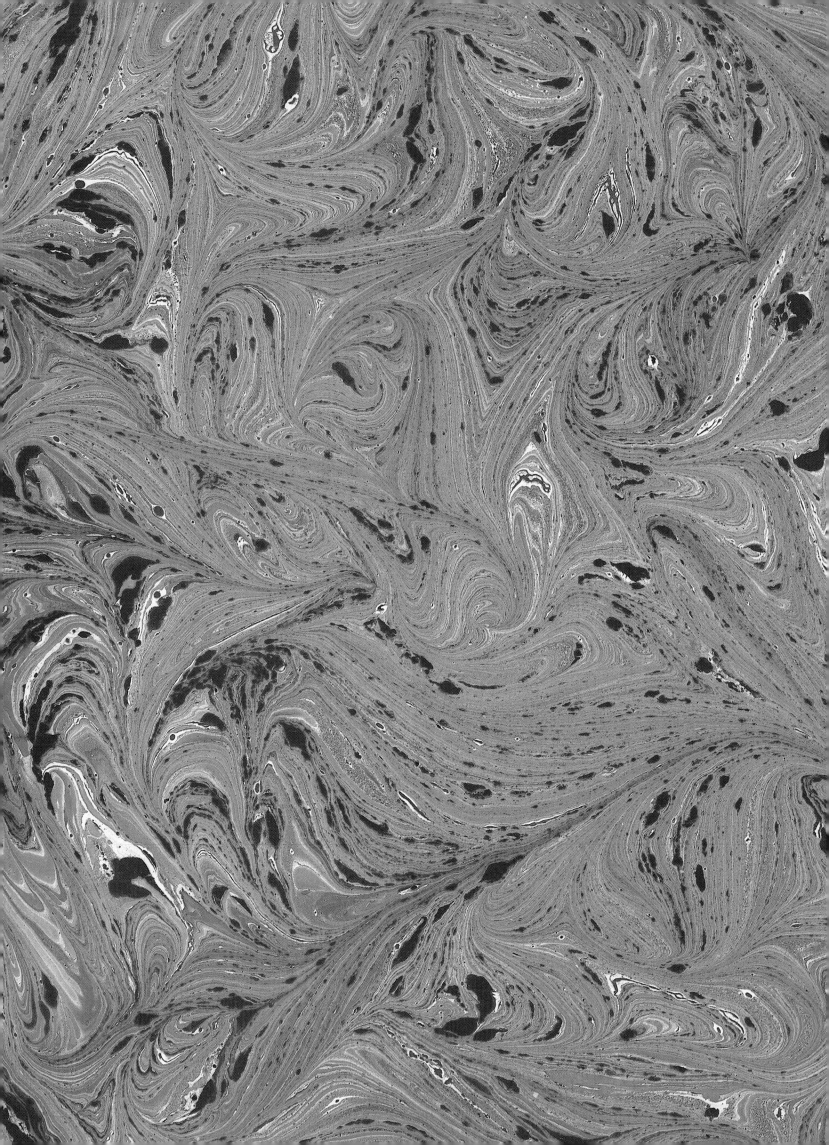

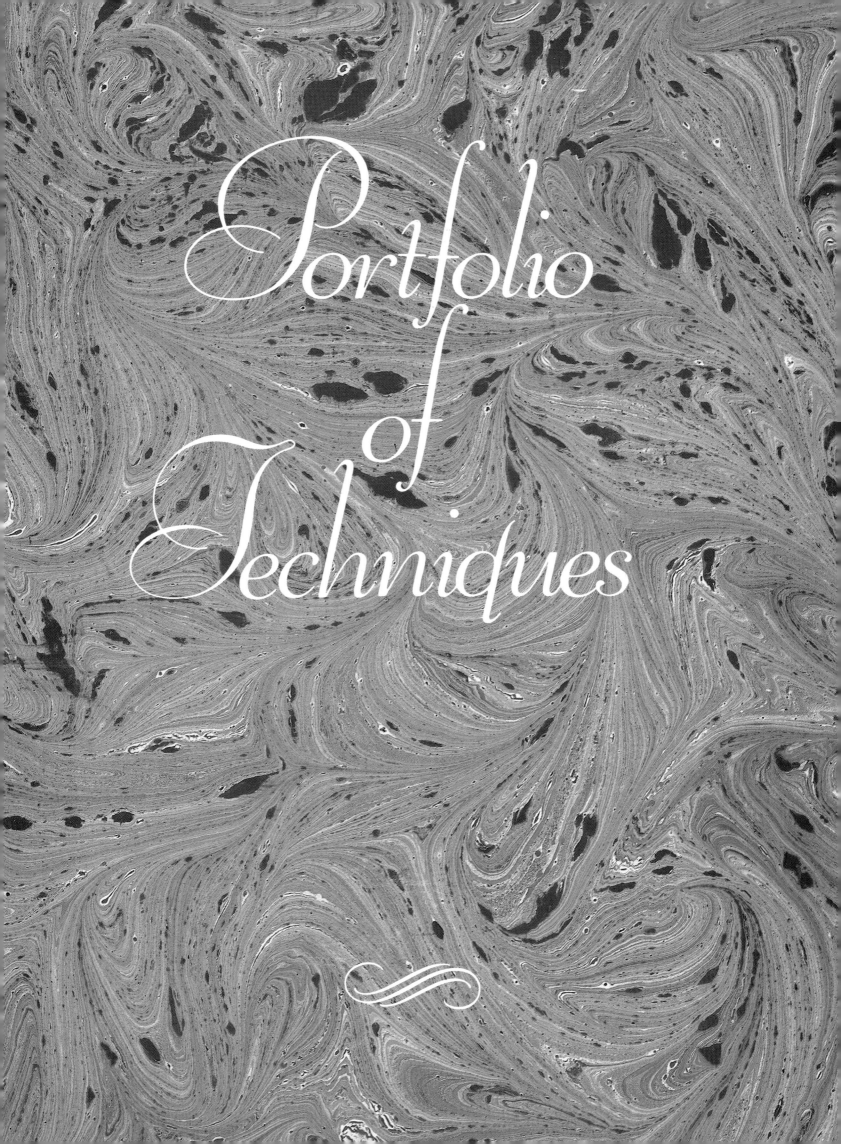

Portfolio
of
Techniques

Working with Greenery

A QUICK WAY TO GIVE A PERSONAL TOUCH TO decorations is to buy fresh fir wreaths and roping and dress them up with fruit, pinecones, ornaments, and bows. If you make your own wreaths and garlands, however, you can work in materials from your garden and the woods that will make your decorations unique. The Southern landscape offers a rich palette of plants—from magnolia, pine, and fir to juniper, palms, nandina, and cherry laurel. Bare branches with berries, such as winterberry and possum haw, can also supply interesting lines and textures.

Most greenery will last longer if you condition it before working with it. Cut the stems on a slant; then place them in buckets of tepid water and leave them in a cool place overnight. Magnolia, holly, hemlock, boxwood, and ivy will all benefit from conditioning, and ivy and boxwood will last much longer if you completely submerge the cuttings in water. Although juniper, pine, arborvitae, and fir may last just as well without conditioning, immersing the branches, foliage and all, in warm water for an hour or so will give the greenery a fresher look.

You can also prolong the life of cut greenery by misting it with water or, even better, spraying it with a floral preservative, which helps slow the plants' loss of moisture. Keeping the room cool will help cut greenery last longer, too.

Remember that some evergreens, such as pine, ooze resins that will leave a sticky residue on woodwork and walls. Avoid hanging pine against a painted wall and protect wood surfaces by spreading a strip of plastic or paper under branches that rest on tables or mantels. (Once you complete the decoration, the protective strip will be hidden.)

Tools of the Trade

HAVING THE RIGHT EQUIPMENT CAN MAKE IT EASIER to achieve professional results in your decorations. In addition to the craft foam and plastic-covered wreath forms shown on pages 185 and 186, the tools pictured above are like those used to create some of the arrangements in this book.

Florists' picks with and without wire are essential to every flower arranger's tool kit. Picks come in several lengths, but the 2¼-inch length will serve most purposes. Sixteen-inch-long hyacinth picks are useful for securing pineapples to a craft foam foundation. For attaching magnolia leaves to craft foam wreaths and badges, you will need fern pins. For making garlands, you can use use either waxed green twine or spool wire.

More specialized products include epergnettes and cages with suction cups. An epergnette is a shallow plastic dish with a grooved projection that fits into a candle holder, turning a candlestick into a

Useful tools for making decorations with greenery and flowers include, clockwise from bottom right, spool wire, waxed twine, florists' picks with and without wire, florists' foam in plastic cages with suction cups, fern pins, an epergnette for turning a candlestick into a vase, florists' foam in a plastic cage on a lightweight hook, clothesline, and garden clippers.

vase. Plastic cages filled with florists' foam and backed with suction cups let you position arrangements on mirrors or windows. After you soak the foam and make the arrangement, you place the suction cup against a smooth, clean surface and pull the plastic handles on the sides, causing the suction cup to adhere. A variation on this is the round plastic cage of florists' foam attached to a hook (it looks like wrought iron but is actually lightweight plastic). This gadget lets you hang an arrangement over a banister, a picture or mirror frame, or a sconce without using nails, wire, or tape.

Lay one or two cuttings along the clothesline and wrap with spool wire. Continue wiring cuttings to the clothesline (above), working all the way around the rope and keeping all stems pointing in the same direction.

The more greenery you use, the thicker the garland will be. Using a variety of evergreens creates an interesting mix of textures and shades of green.

Making a Garland

START WITH A PIECE OF ROPE THE LENGTH YOU WANT the garland to be (clothesline works well) and anchor one end so that you can hold the rope taut as you work. Clip greenery into six-inch-long cuttings. If you cut the stems on a slant, they will disappear more easily among the foliage as you assemble the garland. Wrap one end of the wire near the anchored end of the clothesline to secure it, then lay one or two cuttings along the clothesline and wrap tightly with spool wire (see photograph above). Do not cut the wire. Place another bundle of two or three cuttings on the opposite side of the clothesline and wrap with wire, pulling the wire tightly to secure the cuttings to the rope. Lay a third group along the clothesline so that its foliage generously covers the wire and stems of the first two; spiral the wire down to the stems of this group and wrap them securely to the clothesline.

Continue wiring bundles of cuttings to the clothesline, keeping all stems pointing in the same direction and wrapping the wire as tightly as possible. To make sure the garland is well rounded and full, continue attaching cuttings so that bunches extend to the left, right, and center all the way around the rope. The more greenery you use, the thicker the garland will be.

When you reach the end, hide the stems with bundles of cuttings attached so that the stems point in the opposite direction. Work these stems into the foliage to hide them. To finish, cut off excess clothesline at each end. If any cuttings protrude too much, you can go back and wrap them with more wire higher up along the stem.

Making a Wreath of Mixed Greenery

FOR WREATHS MADE WITH GENEROUS AMOUNTS OF greenery like the one shown here, it is best to use a craft foam form. (The weight of the material is likely to pull a straw wreath form out of shape.) Begin by clipping branchlets and short pieces from branches of evergreens (arborvitae, juniper, and fir were used here).

Attach the cuttings to florists' picks. To make sure the stems are fastened securely, wrap the wire once around the pick and stem; then bring the wire between the stem and the pick and wrap it around the pick, as shown in the photograph (right).

Wrap the wire around both stem and pick several more times; then continue wrapping the wire down the length of the pick (see photograph, below right).

Insert "picked" greenery along the inside, outside, and down the center of a craft foam wreath form (see photograph, opposite above). Work in the same direction all the way around the wreath and insert the picks at an angle to the craft foam form. As you insert stems along the top of the form, angle them to the left, right, and center, so that the finished wreath will have a balanced fullness.

Using mixed greenery yields a rich variety of textures and shades of green. A wreath of a single material, such as fir, juniper, or boxwood, creates a more uniform background for fruits, nuts, and other embellishments.

To secure the greenery so that it will not slip off the pick, wrap the wire once around both pick and stem, then come between the two and wrap the wire around the pick.

Then wrap the wire around both stem and pick and continue wrapping the wire down the length of the pick.

Insert cuttings at an angle to the wreath form and stagger their placement along the top, inside, and outside of the form.

Work in the same direction all the way around the form. After you finish, you can tidy up the wreath, if necessary, by snipping off any pieces of greenery that are too long.

Making a Magnolia Wreath

START WITH A PLASTIC-COVERED STRAW WREATH form (or you can use a craft foam wreath). The magnolia leaves should be fairly uniform in size. Polish them with a soft cloth or an old piece of wool to give them a soft sheen. For a higher gloss, spray them with furniture polish or wipe them with vegetable oil. Then begin by covering the outside edge of the form with the longest leaves, using fern pins to secure them. Overlap the stem of the first leaf with the tip of the next and use a single fern pin to hold both in place. After the outside edge of the wreath is covered, pin individual leaves to the top, staggering them along the form and angling one to the inside, one to the outside, and one along the center (see photograph at top right). For a large wreath, position the leaves at a forty-five-degree angle to the form; for a smaller one, secure the leaves at a more acute angle.

Also insert the pin at an angle, rather than straight down into the wreath (see photograph at right). Work in this manner all the way around the wreath. To finish, tuck the stems of the last leaves under the tips of the first ones.

Cover the outside edge of the wreath form with magnolia leaves, then pin leaves to the top of the form so that they point alternately to the inside and to the outside of the form.

Place the third leaf on top of the first two so that it covers their stems and secure it with a fern pin pushed in at an angle to the form.

Continue pinning leaves to the inside, outside, and center of the form, overlapping the leaves and varying the angles slightly for a more graceful shape. When you reach the end, lift the tips of the first leaves and secure the stems of the last leaves under them.

Making a Badge of Fruit and Greenery

THE EASIEST FOUNDATION TO WORK WITH FOR A badge is craft foam. It comes in sheets that are two inches thick, one foot wide, and three feet long, so you can use the entire sheet for a large badge or cut pieces for the size you need. Round the corners by cutting them off at an angle with a paring knife; then sand the cut edges smooth by rubbing them against another piece of craft foam.

To make a hanger for the badge, push a sixteen-inch-long hyacinth pick through the craft foam block (see photograph, below left), positioning it toward the back and near the top of the block so that the weight of the fruit and greenery will be balanced properly. Cut the pick if necessary so that only about one-half inch protrudes from each side of the craft foam. Wrap #20-gauge florists' wire around both ends to form a loop for hanging.

Cover the outside edge of the craft foam with magnolia leaves, overlapping stems and tips and securing them with fern pins pushed straight into the craft foam. Then pin leaves to the front of the badge in a fan shape. Continue working down the badge, overlapping the edges of the leaves and finish with a fan shape at the opposite end (see photograph, below right).

Insert fruit on florists' picks, pushing the sharp end of the pick through the magnolia leaves and into the craft foam at an angle (see page 188). In the badge shown here, lemons, limes, and an apple are used to create the pattern of color. To position the topmost lemon, a florists' pick is inserted into the end of the fruit instead of the side, so that the lemon can extend beyond the edge of the craft foam.

Finish by wiring sprigs of boxwood to florists' picks and tucking them in around the fruit. Cluster two or three small sprigs on each pick and strip the bottom leaves from the stems so that wiring them to the pick will be easier and less bulky.

Push a hyacinth pick through the craft foam block so that about one-half inch protrudes on each side. Wrap florists' wire around each end to form a hanger.

Attach magnolia leaves to the craft foam block to form a fan shape at each end.

Use florists' picks to secure fruit to the craft foam block. Make a cluster of three lemons at the center for a focal point. Extend the line above and below with more fruit.

Fill in around the fruit with boxwood wired to florists' picks.

The finished badge is symmetrical and formal. Mist daily with water to keep greenery looking fresh.

How to Add Nuts to Wreaths and Garlands

CLUSTERS OF ENGLISH WALNUTS ADD VARIETY IN scale and texture to wreaths and garlands of greenery and fruit. The usual method of attaching them involves drilling holes in the shells and inserting wires, but here is a simpler alternative. Cut old hosiery (the nude color works best) into three- or four-inch squares. Place a nut inside a square of fabric and pull the nylon tightly around the base of nut. Using a florists' pick with wire, wrap the wire tightly around the nylon. The wire is long enough to attach two or three nuts to the same pick (see foreground of photograph) to create a nut cluster. An even easier method, of course, is to attach the nuts with a hot-glue gun.

English walnuts can be attached singly or in pairs, using hosiery and florists' picks or hot glue. (The pinecone roses can be made by cutting the tops off of pinecones. Wrap wire around the bottom layer of scales and twist the ends around a florists' pick to secure the rose to the wreath.)

An easy way to add nuts to wreaths and garlands is to cover them with a scrap of nylon hosiery pulled tightly over the nut and wired to a florists' pick.

Making a Candlestick Arrangement

AN EPERGNETTE LETS YOU MAKE ARRANGEMENTS OF fruit and greenery in candlesticks or candelabra, like the ones shown on page 149. This shallow plastic container holds a block of florists' foam (secured with florists' tape), and a grooved projection on the bottom of the epergnette fits into the candle cup (see photograph, right).

To make an arrangement of pineapple, boxwood, and nandina berries, begin by inserting stems of galax around the rim of the container to hide the epergnette. Then position six-inch picks at each corner and in the center of the florists' foam to hold the pineapple (see photograph, below right). If you insert these picks first, you can then work the boxwood stems in around them and not be concerned about disturbing the boxwood when you position the pineapple.

Clip boxwood into four- to six-inch-long sprigs and wire the sprigs to florists' picks. (Wiring them will be easier if you strip the bottom leaves from the cuttings first.) Insert the cuttings so that those near the top of the florists' foam reach upward, those near the bottom angle downward, and those around the middle extend outward. This will give the boxwood collar a pleasing fullness.

Using an ice pick, make a hole in the bottom of the pineapple; then force the fruit onto the five picks in the florists' foam. Make sure the fruit is upright and perfectly centered on the florists' foam. Otherwise, it may be out of balance and cause the arrangement to fall over.

Fill in around the pineapple with boxwood, and add small clusters of nandina berries to finish.

Secure florists' foam in the epergnette with florists' tape, then position the epergnette in the candlestick.

Cover the rim of the container with galax leaves and position florists' picks at the corners and center to hold the pineapple. Sprig boxwood into the sides of the florists' foam.

Make a hole in the core of the pineapple, then push the fruit down onto the picks, being careful to center it precisely so that the weight will be balanced. Add nandina berries for color.

Credits

PHOTOGRAPHERS

Jack Alterman, 158 bottom
Paul G. Beswick, 134-35, 159
Doug Castanedo, 44, 45
Van Chaplin, 110, 111 right, 112, 113, 128 top left and bottom right, 131 right, 138 bottom left and right, 140, 148 bottom right, 156 left
Gary Clark, 20, 21, 22, 23, 24-25, 26, 27, 42, 43, 58, 59, 60, 61, 114, 115, 141 left, 145 right, 146 bottom left, 147 bottom left, 163, 173 top left and right
Cheryl Sales Dalton, ii, iv, 98, 99, 100, 101, 102, 103
Leslie Wright Dow, 157 bottom, 160, 161
Colleen Duffey, 124-25, 126 top and bottom right, 129 left, 142-43, 173 bottom, 189 right
Patrick Elam, 46, 47, 48, 49, 126 left, 127, 155
Anne Gunnerson, 13, 14, 15, 18-19, 148 left
Richard Haggerty, 133 bottom, 136 bottom left, 139 bottom left, 146 top and right, 149, 153 bottom, 156 right, 157 top, 171, 172 top left
Hickey-Robertson, 128 top right
Steve Hogben, 54-55, 56, 57, 147 bottom, 174 bottom, 177
Mac Jamieson, 132 left
Gene Johnson, 86-87, 88, 89, 90, 91, 92, 93, 94-95, 96, 97, 153 top, 158 top, 166-67
Louis Joyner, 133 top
78, 79, 80, 81, 82-83, 84, 85, 104, 105, 106-107, 108, 109, 129 right, 132 right, 168, 174 top left and right
Sylvia Martin, 28, 29, 30, 31, 32, 33, 137 bottom left, 138 top, 139 bottom
Beth Maynor, viii, 12, 16, 17, 34-35, 36-37, 130, 131 left, 136 right, 137
top left and right, 144, 145 left, 147 right, 154
John Nation, 50-51, 52, 53
John O'Hagan, 118, 119, 120, 121, 136 top left, 152, 176, 180-81, 182, 183, 184, 185, 186, 187, 188, 189 left, 190, 191
Howard Lee Puckett, 111 left, 116, 117
Michael Rivers, 38-39, 40, 41, 169, 172 bottom
David Schilling, 139 right, 141 right, 148 top right

PHOTOSTYLISTS

Nancy Ingram, 86-87, 88, 89, 90, 91, 92, 93, 94-95, 96, 97, 153 top, 158 top, 166-67
Joetta Moulden, cover, vi, ix, 62, 63, 64, 65, 66, 67, 70, 71, 72, 73, 74, 75, 76, 77, 78, 79, 80, 81, 82-83, 84, 85, 105, 106-107, 108, 109, 129 right, 132 right, 168, 174 top left and right
Catherine S. Stoddard, 180-81, 182, 183, 184, 185, 186, 187, 188, 189, 190, 191

DESIGNERS AND HOMEOWNERS

Following are designers and homeowners not credited elsewhere.

David Alexander, Baltimore, Maryland, 141 left, 147 bottom left, 163
Mr. and Mrs. Harry M. Ford, Jr.
The American College for the Applied Arts ASID Student Chapter, Atlanta, Georgia, 174 bottom right
Mr. and Mrs. M. E. Costello
Sheldon Anderson, Charlottesville, Virginia, 124-25, 129 left
Mr. and Mrs. Wendell W. Wood
Jim Bagwell Associates and Susie Kay, Dallas, Texas, 131 right
Mr. and Mrs. Jim Milner
Carolyn W. Clark, Atlanta, Georgia, 56 right
Peggy Conway and Betty Jo Cowin, Birmingham, Alabama, 43 top
Fred R. Cannon, Jr., Brooklyn, New York, 164, 165 right, 170
Sharyl Redfern Davis and Carlos Gonzalez, San Antonio, Texas, 128 top right (Mr. and Mrs. W. Randolph Davis)
Becky Dossey, Houston, Texas, 168
Mary P. Elam, ASID, Greensboro, North Carolina, 146 top and right, 157
Jenkins/Eliason Interiors, Louisville, Kentucky
Kentucky Governor's Mansion, 50-51, 52, 53
Sandy Metts, 136 top left
Mr. and Mrs. John Y. Brown, 152, 176
James Essary Associates, Charlotte, North Carolina, 157 bottom
171 bottom, 172 top right
Mr. and Mrs. Joseph Miller
Dan Flannery, Kansas City, Missouri, 153 top, 158 top, 166-67
Mr. and Mrs. Doug Rose
Ryan Gainey and Leroy Hannah, Atlanta, Georgia, 139 right, 141 right, 148 top right
Mr. and Mrs. R. J. Johnson
Galloway Florists, Houston, Texas, cover and 132 right
Dr. and Mrs. Ralph Ford
Marvin Gardens Patrick, Atlanta, Georgia
Mr. and Mrs. M. E. Costello

Marvin Gardens, 177
Donna Williams
Nancy Gee, Austin, Texas, 140 bottom
Isabel Gordon, Charlottesville, Virginia, 142-43
Dr. and Mrs. A. Nelson Yarbrough
Nancy Gould, ix
Andy Hallock, Charlottesville, Virginia, 173 bottom
Dr. and Mrs. A. Nelson Yarbrough
Daniel M. Hawks, Williamsburg, Virginia, 144 left
Lt. Gen. Mrs. Pat W. Crizer
James Hollingsworth, Charlottesville, Virginia, 126 top and bottom right, 189 right
Mr. and Mrs. Jason I. Eckford
Mrs. Randolph Bolling Hubard, Owings Mills, Maryland, 20, 21, 22, 23
Claude Jones, Williamsburg, Virginia, 130
William K. Murphy
Josephine Jones, Williamsburg, Virginia, top 137
William K. Murphy
Junior Board of Historic Fredericksburg Foundation, Fredericksburg, Virginia
Mr. and Mrs. Christopher M. Hallberg, 131 left
Frank Kimbrough, Roxboro, North Carolina
Mr. and Mrs. R. Daniel Walker, 136 bottom left, 153 bottom
Dr. and Mrs. Thomas Alexander, Roxboro, 171 top left and right
Cliff Lassahn, Baltimore, Maryland, 148 left
Lenox Interiors and Antiques, Atlanta, Georgia, 54-55
Judy Lopp, Associate ASID, Greensboro, North Carolina, 172 top left
Lucille Maloney, Gainesville, Florida, 138 bottom left and right
Memphis Garden Club, 139 bottom left, 150-51
Mobile Chapters of the Daughters of the American Revolution, Mobile, Alabama, 169, 172 bottom (Richards-DAR House)
Ann W. Osteen, Savannah, Georgia, 127 bottom
J. Porter Paul, Winston-Salem, North Carolina, 114, 115, 146 bottom left, 173 top left and right
Lyman Ratcliffe, Houston, Texas, 174 left and top right
Mr. and Mrs. H. L. Simpson
Tucker Renfrow, ISID, Raleigh, North Carolina, 139 top left, 175
Elizabeth Fentress
Meg Rice and Kenzie Hannah, Houston, Texas, 129 right
Mr. and Mrs. Joel Swanson
River Oaks Garden Club, 62, 63, 64, 65, 66, 67
162 top (Mr. and Mrs. James Scott)
Susan Scott, Washington Depot, Connecticut, 137 bottom left, 138 top left,
Gene Shull, Williamsburg, Virginia, 147 right
Mr. and Mrs. William Digges
Jeannie Taylor Sims, ASLA, Savannah, Georgia, 155
Frank Smith and Al Dellinger, Atlanta, Georgia, 56 left
Joe Smith, Nashville, Tennessee, 145 right
Edward H. Springs, ASID, Charlotte, North Carolina, 160, 161
Bob Strother, Cary, North Carolina, 133 bottom, 149, 156 right,
177 top left and right
Mr. and Mrs. Frank Daniels, Raleigh
Dottie Toole, Savannah, Georgia, 127 top (Mr. and Mrs. F. M. Toole)
Eleanor C. Weller, Allied Member ASID, Monkton, Maryland, 134-35, 159
Whippoorwill Co., Atlanta, Georgia, 57
Bill Whisenant, Birmingham, Alabama
Arlington, 43 bottom
Historic Donnelly House and Gardens, 128 bottom right, 148 bottom right
Jan Williams, Fredericksburg, Virginia, 154
Roy Williams, Williamsburg, Virginia, 136 right, 137 right
Dr. and Mrs. Paul Verkuil
Bobb Wirfel, Houston, Texas, vi

The Editors wish to express special appreciation to the following for their assistance: The Junior Board of the Historic Fredericksburg Foundation; the Junior League of Charlottesville; the Green Spring Garden Club of Williamsburg; Peggy Howe, North Carolina Department of Cultural Resources; Carolinas Chapter, American Society of Interior Designers; Mary Cory, curator, William Paca House; Barbara Brand, administrator, Mount Clare; Anne Fox, administrator, Joseph Manigault House; Frankie Hammond-Harwood House; William G. Workman, former administrator, Webb, administrator, Aiken-Rhett House; Ron Singleton, Office of Public Information, and Mrs. William Anderson, Mary Washington College; Abby M. Gilman, historic properties manager, Oakleigh; Dan Brooks, director, Arlington; Ron Strahan, Magnolia Place Inn; Marie Gardner, property manager, Office of Historic Properties, Kentucky Governor's Mansion; Jeanne C. McKeithen, special events coordinator, Stranahan House; Mary Lynne Oglesby, publicity coordinator, The Callanwolde Fine Arts Center; Sandee Chilton, marketing coordinator, Graylyn Conference Center; Nancy Block, former administrator, and Michael K. Brown, curator, The Bayou Bend Collection; Peggy Jo Shaw.

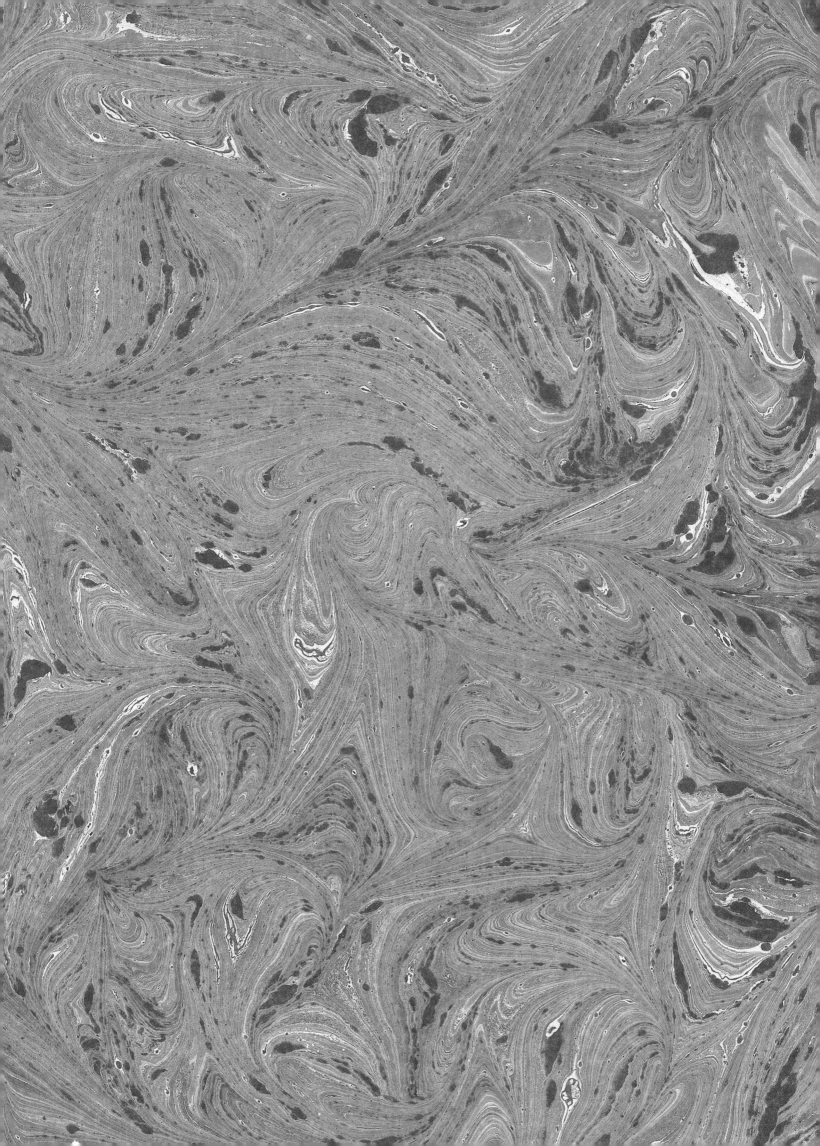